SCIENCE
WORKSHOP

SCIENCE WORKSHOP

WORKSHOP

A Whole Language Approach

Wendy Saul

Jeanne Reardon • Anne Schmidt • Charles Pearce

Dana Blackwood • Mary Dickinson Bird

Heinemann
Portsmouth, NH

Heinemann Educational Books, Inc.
361 Hanover Street   Portsmouth, NH 03801-3912
Offices and agents throughout the world

Page 98: "Five-Step Scientific Method" from *How to Think Like a Scientist* by Stephen P. Kramer. Text copyright © 1987 by Stephen P. Kramer. Reprinted by permission of HarperCollins Publishers.

We wish to thank the children and parents who have given their permission to include material in this book. Every effort has been made to contact the copyright holders for permission to reprint borrowed material where necessary. We regret any oversights that may have occurred and would be happy to rectify them in future printings of this work.

Library of Congress Cataloging-in-Publication Data

Science workshop : a whole language approach / Wendy Saul . . . [et al.].
    p. cm.
   Includes bibliographical references.
   ISBN 0-435-08336-8
   1. Science–Study and teaching (Elementary)–United States.
   2. Language experience approach in education–United States.
   3. Teaching–Aids and devices. I. Saul, Wendy.
   LB1585.3.S36   1993
   372.3′5′044–dc20
                                92-21468
                                CIP

Designed by Janet Patterson
Cover drawings by Emma Tobin
Printed in the United States of America
93 94 95 96 97   7 6 5 4 3 2 1

Contents

Acknowledgments

The material in this volume is based upon work supported by the National Science Foundation under grant number TPE-8955187. Any opinions, findings, and conclusions or recommendations expressed in this material are those of the authors and do not necessarily reflect the views of the National Science Foundation.

Contributors

Wendy Saul, an Associate Professor of Education at the University of Maryland, Baltimore County, is Director of the Elementary Science Integration Project. Books include *Science Fare* (Harper and Row, 1986) and (with Sybille Jagusch) *Vital Connections: Children, Science, and Books* (Library of Congress, 1991; Heinemann, 1992). She is the Associate Editor of *The New Advocate.*

Jeanne Reardon teaches primary grades in the Montgomery County Public Schools, Maryland. She often writes about and makes presentations based on her classroom research. Her articles have appeared in *The New Advocate, Vital Connections: Children, Science, and Books* (Library of Congress, 1991; Heinemann, 1992), and *Assessment and Evaluation in Whole Language Classrooms* (Christopher Gordon, 1991).

Anne Schmidt has been a teacher with the Baltimore City Public School System for the past twenty-three years. Having had experience at every elementary grade level, she is now involved in developing strategies to improve the language skills of urban students. She also works free-lance gathering children's writings for the *Baltimore Sun.*

Charles Pearce chose to be a teacher after fifteen years in industry. He teaches fifth grade in Carroll County, Maryland.

Dana Blackwood is an elementary school teacher in the Fairfax County Public School System. During her twenty-five years of teaching, Ms. Blackwood has taught children in grades two, four, five, and six.

Mary Dickinson Bird developed and taught school outreach programs for Boston's Museum of Science, and served as a science specialist in one of the Boston Public Schools. She now teaches at the University of Maryland, Baltimore County and at Trinity College in Washington, D.C. Ms. Bird is the principal author of *Science for Children: Resources for Teachers,* published by the National Science Resources Center.

1 Wendy Saul

Science Workshop

Fifteen years ago one would have been surprised to walk into an American elementary school classroom and find children busily engaged in a wide variety of literacy-related activities—drawing, making lists, reading alone, taking notes, drafting, revising, conferring with a teacher or classmate, reading aloud with a friend, or publishing their own books. Today, thanks to the work of Donald Graves, Donald Murray, Lucy Calkins, Nancie Atwell, Ken and Yetta Goodman, and the many teachers who have enlivened and developed their ideas in classrooms, "workshops" are considered a legitimate, even an ordinary, part of the language curriculum. *Science Workshop* is an attempt to bring some of the wisdom of the whole language workshop to bear on science instruction. It is also an attempt to tell how a community of teachers, gathered under the banner of the "Elementary Science Integration Project," adapted whole language methods and concerns to science teaching. In so doing we hope to help other "whole language teachers" see that much of what they have come to understand about working with children will serve them well as they go about teaching science.

While reading the previous paragraph you may have noted my shorthand for describing a whole language class. Basically, I listed a set of activities, which implied a knowledge of reading and writing process, which in turn presupposed an attitude about what kind of learning environment best serves children. While the hope is that this shorthand for a whole language classroom is predicated on an underlying commitment to a theory of language and curriculum as well as a familiarity with certain developmental issues, this is often not the case. Books touted by publishers as exemplars of whole language line the display aisles at professional meetings, yet few publishers seem to understand or represent the teaching of reading or writing as process.

Science activities also signal attitudes about the way knowledge is conceptualized and the way children learn. We tend to think of a classroom in which students are busily engaged in the processes of science—observing, measuring, testing, and so on—as one that embodies a different attitude toward the study of science from one in which children take turns reading from a textbook. Those who associate science with doing and discovery seek programs and materials rich in opportunities for hands-on work. But good science instruction is about more than appropriate materials and activities, just as whole language is about more than big books and classroom publishing opportunities. Although an ideal classroom will have such materials available to children, the heart of the workshop is located in an attitude toward and an interpretation of activity. That is why this book is not about any one set of science texts, activities, or modules.

Progressive science educators have been instrumental in guiding their districts away from textbook-based programs to hands-on units. Typically, boxes of materials arrive in the classroom and can be kept and used there for eight to twelve weeks. I tend to think of these programs in the same way I think about school breakfasts—they are a good idea, and should be supported. On the other hand, such programs do not provide total "science nutrition." Teachers and children, maintaining the suggested pace, proceed through a carefully sequenced set of activities, often feeling like victims of the fast-forward button on the VCR; such units ensure neither the children's interest nor the kind of conversation that fosters inquiry and investigation. The kits may spark questions, but leave little curricular space or time for personal exploration and investment.

Less progressive school districts still depend largely on textbooks for science instruction or, in some instances, offer no science at all. Although this is certainly demoralizing, it may be possible for teachers in these situations to add a science workshop on their own or to teach a parallel science program, in which the science workshop is offered sometime in the school day not already designated for the science textbook. Many pioneering whole language teachers moved reading and writing workshops in right alongside their basal programs, and it may not be impossible to take on science in the same way. It is the teacher who enables children to find the time or space to think hard, to explore, to grow as independent learners.

A Brief History and Status Report

This introductory chapter seeks to make explicit the way science instruction benefits from the perspectives of teachers committed to whole language. But while the chapters that follow build from experiences in individual classrooms, this chapter starts from a view outside the classroom and seeks to identify overall patterns. In that spirit it seems useful to describe the present state of science education and to consider our history—how we got where we are.

The launch of Sputnik in 1957 may have had a more profound effect on American science instruction than on space exploration. Although significant national resources had already been dedicated to finding ways to improve science education, this event made the need for more and better instruction obvious to an informed citizenry. The approach taken in the 1950s and 1960s is one that will sound familiar to reading/writing process teachers. Curriculum planners went out and asked practicing scientists not only what they did but also what habits of mind and experiences led them to become scientists. The answers that emerged—scientists observed, counted, made informed guesses, tested those guesses—became the processes teachers familiar with programs like Elementary Science Study (ESS), Science Curriculum Improvement Study (SCIS), and Science, A Process Approach (SAPA) immediately recognize.

In many ways these units were wonderful. They asserted, by their form and content, that science was not a static body of knowledge that could be codified in a textbook. Instead science was an activity that built upon inquiry and imagination. Children were not taught a step-by-step approach, a single way to obtain a given correct answer, but instead were challenged to come up with a variety of approaches and explanations. In order to keep teachers from giving away answers and to invite their participation as fellow travelers, little direction was given. The teachers and the children were out there exploring (and sometimes floundering) together.

Although this sounded good in theory, most teachers, already insecure about their science knowledge, didn't seem to enjoy this role at all. Moreover, these units suffered from materials problems: teachers were often uncomfortable managing the number of things required for each lesson; the materials themselves were often missing or damaged; and local troubleshooters were hard to find.

In the twenty years that followed, two basic responses to the problems that marked these programs surfaced: (1) the hands-on units were deemed a disaster and either (a) the units were put away in favor of a textbook or (b), more likely, the science program was abandoned entirely or (2) school districts sought local ways to make hands-on units more "teacher friendly." In the latter case, handbooks with clearer directions were developed, and local shops for replenishing materials were created. Much of the current, renewed energy being directed toward science education builds upon this second approach; national efforts now focus on helping large school systems promote and manage hands-on, modular programs.

All of us involved in this book recognize that good science instruction means hands-on work. But we also worry, collectively and individually, about the limitations of large-scale solutions. Teachers and school systems eager to solve the "science problem" take hands-on curriculums as *the* answer and stop thinking about a next step, about ways that the kit programs fall short, about the excitement of extended study.

The "thinking large" approach appears to address the needs of more children and teachers and does ensure that some good science instruction will be offered to all. But for those of us who wish to see teachers as individuals who bring their own skills, questions, and knowledge to children, these large-scale programs are only a "jump start." Schools, we believe, need to benefit from local resources, both natural and human. By expanding upon the uniform scope and sequence program, we seek to bring children's questions and concerns closer to the center of science learning; as a result, classroom science instruction may become more idiosyncratic, less uniform.

In short, those who value teachers as decision makers and learners need to insist that these hands-on packages are a beginning, not an end point. The forty-minute science segment offered twice a week, if it is truly engaging, needs to spill over into math and reading and recess. Similarly, the questions that arise in art class as colors dribble and sculptures fall need to be recognized as science. This book, then, is about science as a way of thinking, a way of viewing the world, an approach to problem solving.

What Is a Workshop?

Walking into the sixth-grade area, it is difficult to spot a teacher. Finally I find her, belly down on the carpeted floor, watching with three children as mealworms scurry in a shoe box. "Which colors do they like?" asks one young man. After listening to a three-minute discussion on "how you tell," the teacher interrupts with a question: "When you set up this experiment, how will you decide whether the mealworms are being given a 'fair trial'?" Seeing that the discussion is again underway, she jots something on a "sticky note" and moves on to talk with a girl who is looking at a live frog and comparing it with the glossy color photograph in the trade book she holds.

"Ms. Reeves, this frog doesn't look the same as the one in the picture."

"Good observation," the teacher replies. "Why not make a list of all those points that you notice are different?"

The teacher proceeds from group to group, stopping to chat with individuals, taking an occasional note. Only two of the groups are working with the same materials; one group is helping prove a "theory" another group has decided is ready to be tested elsewhere. My overwhelming sense, as an observer, is that this classroom is a busy place.

After allowing the students about thirty minutes for investigation, the teacher gives a five-minute warning, reminding them to log in the day's activities. The class is then told they will meet to discuss the science activities right after lunch.

The above scenario is an example of a science workshop as we use the term in this book. What makes the science classrooms described in the following pages workshops? What makes them like one another? What makes them like their counterparts in reading or writing? Although these are clearly complex questions, there appear to be certain characteristics that at least in part define the workshop as we know it: authenticity, autonomy, and community.

Authenticity

Authenticity is key to any workshop model. In language arts we talk about the importance of children writing from their own experiences and imaginations. Similarly, we see children's trade books, literature written by authors who understand the power and beauty of language, as the basis of a good reading program. In sum, a workshop-based language arts approach is built on the study and appreciation of masters of language, and it seeks to foster similar practices among children.

Authenticity is also an issue in science. A science workshop needs to foster the kind of thinking engaged in by scientists, those people who find pleasure in the systematic study of our world. As such, an understanding of what scientists do—how they ask questions, explore phenomena, speculate about why certain things happen, and arrive at convincing, reasonable answers—needs to be an essential piece of any science workshop. A general understanding of these processes is well within the grasp of elementary school teachers and their students.

Authenticity should also be a feature of the subjects to be investigated. Children need to be working on problems that they recognize as personally challenging and that make sense. Although teachers or books may be instrumental in generating an initial interest in a topic, students must play a major role in determining the path for pursuing that inquiry.

Those familiar with the power of literature to nurture reading and writing abilities can appreciate how children seek to understand the way the world works, both as lovers of knowledge and as participants in experiments that result in satisfying explanations. Science trade books—literature that tells stories about scientific events, recounts and explains facts, or proposes activities—offer another authentic science voice in the classroom.

Authenticity is also evident in the way workshop teachers and children relate to one another. Children's ideas are respected and credited, and, in the best lessons, teachers and children share their curiosities. Workshop talk feels more like a professional meeting than the kind of parroting and cajoling dialogue that results when students are asked to guess the answer the teacher wants. This is not to suggest that such formats are always inappropriate in teaching science, but we need to recognize that teacher-centered and teacher-controlled lessons are not components of process-oriented workshops.

Autonomy

Autonomy is another feature that characterizes the workshop. Student authors, like their professional counterparts, take on both the freedom and the responsibilities associated with trying to produce excellent work. In this sense there are many decisions to be made: given the general parameters established by the teacher, how will I go about my work? with whom do I wish to work? how do I know when I'm doing a good job? what do I do next? The science and writing workshops have much in common—both seek to help children become more adept at learning on their own and more able to engage in sustained and focused thought.

The other significant feature of the science workshop has to do with time. Units that come prepackaged from the school district arrive and depart on specific dates. This means that children and teachers must fit their explorations into discrete and relatively short time periods. Science workshop involves more time than the discrete science lesson, but the time it takes can also be counted as writing, reading, art, or social studies.

The authors of this book are thoroughly committed to the notion that children need time to "mess around" in science. Generally, young people benefit from repeating the same activity several times, in just the same way they enjoy reading a book or singing a song again and again. The repeated investigation convinces children of one of the major tenets of science—that the same procedure with the same materials leads to the same result. Kit programs by and large do little to encourage such repetition because it seems less efficient and economical.

We all need time to worry ideas into place. An argument could be made that *not* giving children that time may finally be our undoing. If young people are to understand science as reasoned analysis rather than as doctrine, they need to believe in what they see and do, not take it on faith that what their teacher says is correct. A teacher, under pressure to "move on," traditionally gives up by telling children the "answer" and having them repeat it either orally or on a test. And children, eager to please, repeat what the teacher deems worthy of a good grade. In so doing young people learn that science is a body of knowledge to be memorized rather than understood, an arena where curiosity and persistence count for little.

Because workshop interests and plans vary, students are often engaged in a wide variety of activities. Workshop teachers have learned to be comfortable changing gears and keeping track of such dissimilarities. Even when a project starts from a similar premise or question—which fabric is more waterproof? what do we know about a hermit crab's claw?—diversity of response is not only expected but encouraged.

Community

A sense of community is also central to the workshop. Ideally, classrooms are places where teachers and children work as a unique community of thinkers. One year looks different from another, not just because another curriculum package was adopted on the district level, but because each year teachers and children come with new thoughts and experiences to share. To succeed in a workshop, children and teachers must be aware of the resources available in the classroom community—who writes fantasy and who reads biography, who spells well and who never forgets her homework. In a workshop children are encouraged to use each other and collaboration is invited.

Community is also evident in the standards students set for their work. Because they see themselves as practicing authors or scientists, their "results" are presented to and evaluated by peers. Questions such as the one posed by teacher Jeanne Reardon ("What evidence do my first graders find convincing in evaluating data?") become logical in a workshop environment where sharing is an ordinary and important part of the day.

There are, however, significant differences in the intellectual rules set by a science community and a language community. Whereas emotion is often central to literary response, in science one actively seeks to separate emotional reactions from empirical evidence. In science, if there is a choice between believing what seems entirely logical and clearly stated and believing the data—the concrete results of an experiment—it is incumbent upon the science student to opt for the data. The point here is that an experiment or explanation is not valued because everyone in the class agrees that it is correct. Rather, the power of an idea is evidenced in repetition—will it work that way every time? can I predict which flowers these bees are more likely to visit? No one, on the other hand, would say, This is an excellent poem because I can write one just like it, or, This book is wonderful because I knew exactly what would happen to the protagonist.

But this does *not* mean that emotion is absent from the science workshop. Children and adults can learn to appreciate skepticism in a wholehearted way. Moreover, they can be impressed, emotionally impressed, with good questions and interesting findings. In developing hypotheses, gut feelings do count; there are many famous stories about a scientist working doggedly on a problem day in and day out only to have the solution come suddenly in a dream. The problems and solutions of science can mean enough to penetrate an investigator's subconscious; in such instances the distinctions between cognitive and affective responses become blurred. An atmosphere that supports the rethinking of ideas and invites an appreciation of problem solving is one that fosters science as well as language learning.

Cooperative learning strategies and an assigned sharing/celebration time are often regular features of the process-oriented classroom. But in a successful workshop, sharing and cooperation go far beyond the technical, sometimes formulaic exercises designed to model caring and trust, encouragement and appreciation. Through the workshop, children and teachers seek to help one another grow, learn, and share the frustration and delight of working hard. Whereas in many classrooms children come to value others' failure as a way to buoy their own success, in a workshop excellence and even improvement are viewed as both personal and community triumphs.

In speaking primarily to the similarities between a reading/writing workshop and a science workshop I do not wish to ignore the differences. I believe, for instance, that most teachers have a clearer understanding of the way that developmental issues are played out in the learning of language than in the learning of science. Also, while the study of reading or writing begins with natural, oral language, there are many questions about how the languages of science, both words and numbers, play off one another. Further, ordinary adult language activities—reading a novel or writing a well-crafted letter—lead teachers to believe that they can teach reading and writing. However, adult science—its precision, stature, and distance from everyday experience—leads teachers to believe that they have nothing to offer children in science. We take exception to that.

Using Ourselves

Teachers who feel insecure with science generally begin by thinking how different science is from anything they know. Interestingly, the list of what they don't know tends to focus on content: I don't know about batteries, I don't know the difference between metamorphic and igneous rock, I don't know about the phases of the moon. In an attempt to empower science-phobic teachers, science educators have tended to focus on teaching content—"Here's a hands-on activity you can do with children," says the workshop leader, and teachers, eager for something that children will enjoy and learn from, leave the workshop happy. The problem, of course, is that in their hearts they don't believe that what they can do is really science. They are still burdened by the weight of all they don't know and are left wondering what will happen when children need something substantive and information based. Real science people, they believe, are a fountain of facts.

Such opinions are reinforced in a variety of ways. Scientists and science educators regularly express something between distress and disgust about how few college science courses elementary school teachers typically take. And the teachers, thinking back to that freshman biology or chemistry class, ponder all the courses in which they did not enroll. Simply to keep up with the four units in the third-grade curriculum they should have taken geology, physics, paleontology, and electrical engineering.

Popular culture also contributes to this feeling of desperation that the teacher with a meager science background feels. In a society that recognizes and values expertise, we know that scientists are the ones to turn to for specialized information and critical, informed judgments. A team of scientists is called in to discuss global warming, world hunger, the reasons the spaceship Challenger exploded. Of course, these aren't the same teams of scientists, but somehow that fact isn't made clear. My husband—who has a Ph.D. in chemistry, is an amateur astronomer, and writes about environmental issues—doesn't know enough geology to teach a standard fourth-grade unit. The difference is that he would approach the task as interesting, and he would be confident about his ability to connect what he already knows to the subject at hand.

I suspect that additional coursework, though potentially helpful, is not the key to more and better elementary school science. Nor is it in our interest to turn teachers into "resource junkies," people in search of more and better materials and activities. Rather, if we seek real change in attitudes toward science, we need to begin with the strengths teachers have and with their ability to locate help when necessary.

An example might prove useful here. A science resource specialist in an elementary school arranged for the third graders to dissect fish, one fish per child. The activity began in the regular classroom: twenty-six children gathered around the chalkboard and the resource teacher asked them what they expected to find. Three children eagerly answered questions and another four or five seemed to be actively listening. Then the children followed the science specialist into the "science" room, where the fish were distributed.

The science teacher had assembled a team of adults—herself, the regular teacher, an aide, and a parent with a Ph.D. in neuroscience. The children were divided into groups, and each adult was kept busy attending to six or seven youngsters trying to use knives. When all the fish were opened, the adults helped children identify lungs and gills, scales and fins.

Two teacher observers (let's call them X and Y) commented on this event, which by all accounts went well. Ms. X focused almost entirely on the kind and amount of information the science specialist and scientist had at their disposal. In this hierarchy the science teacher had the greatest knowledge, the scientist was second, the aide (a recreational fisherman) was third, and the regular teacher had the least information to share with the students. Observer X determined not only that she knew less than the classroom teacher, but also that she was put off by the slimy innards. This observation provided confirmation—living proof—that teacher observer X would never be able to teach science.

The second observer, Ms. Y, "used herself" in her analysis. To begin, she noticed the general lack of participation in the precutting phase. As a writing teacher Ms. Y realized that some sort of "write to know" activity—drawing a picture, making a list, or collaborating with a friend on a short discussion about what might be inside—would have involved every child in the class, and set each up better to appreciate the hands-on activity.

Second, because she and the children in her own classroom were comfortable with the idea that everyone needn't be doing the same thing at the same time, she realized that the hands-on work could have taken place in the regular classroom, thus reducing the number of adults needed and making the dissection part of the daily routine rather than a special activity.

Finally, Ms. Y felt confident that she could find trade books and reference materials that would assist her in answering children's questions, and that she needn't become an expert in ichthyology in order to undertake the dissection activity. In short, the teacher who had the confidence to use herself left the demonstration lesson ready and able to take on this activity and ones like it. The teacher awed by expertise, on the other hand, felt confirmed in her insecurity; she concluded that it was better to stay away from what she didn't know well.

This book assumes that teachers familiar with the workshop model have a great resource for building on and connecting with children's natural interest in science. The remainder of this book makes some explicit procedural suggestions and shows how a knowledge of process in reading and writing can be used as the scaffold for helping children investigate their natural world.

What *Do* We Know?

Teachers of reading and writing need to begin with what they know and try to generalize that knowledge in ways that apply to the learning of science. First, there must be engaging materials. To teach language arts, I need books: books that are familiar and speak to the experiences of children in my class; books that are unfamiliar and challenge children to view the world differently; books that children can take and read independently; books that are best shared. I want books that I as a teacher enjoy reading so that I can learn with the children; if a book becomes stale for me, I am less able to share my passion for words and ideas. I choose books with children, not for children, and as a reader adviser look for connections between what has interested them—subjects, authors, feelings—and the available literature. If I have read the book before, I am better able to recommend and discuss it, but even if my recommendation is "blind," I still feel comfortable asking authentic, generic questions.

That same confidence needs to characterize science instruction. Most teachers, in thinking about science, begin by considering the subject matter that will become the focus of study. Are there certain topics that provide richer fields for exploration than others? Authors of science curriculums have also started here, with *what* to teach. But it is important to recognize that the audience for regional or national kit programs may be different from a particular class with a particular teacher (i.e., you).

I recommend that you begin a science workshop by focusing not on the subject (which leads quickly away from what you know), but rather on the experiences you share with the children in your charge. Start with local interest—the rain on a window, a question about what makes some balls roll faster than others. Start with concrete experience—a praying mantis found on the way to school, a flower in the schoolyard that isn't immediately recognized. Start always with a curiosity or a concern, never with an abstract concept like molecules or fission that cannot be sensed and tested directly. Bernie Zubrowski (1990), children's author and a physicist by training, talks about the importance of beginning with materials that have an intrinsic interest. His own work with balloons, cars, mirrors, clocks, drinking-straw constructions, and bubbles provides a model for challenges that can be undertaken in a workshop setting.

As in the writing or reading workshop, materials are important but needn't be expensive or hard to find. Through the years, as reading and writing teachers, we have developed attentive eyes—we see natural examples of reading and writing and glorious speech everywhere we look. Science workshop teachers, with attentive eyes, will find that science materials and possibilities abound. But, as James Rutherford (1991), chief education officer of the American Association for the Advancement of Science, has pointed out, science is not in the materials but in the perspective one takes towards those materials, in the questions one asks and answers about those materials.

> Seashells, for example, are not science; they are just things. Admiring their beauty is not science. Drawing them carefully may or may not be science depending on its purpose. Captur-

ing their beauty is a wonderful thing to do, but it is not
science. Trying to figure out things about seashells: that is
science. But a child doesn't care what you call it as long as it's
interesting. Do spiral shells always spiral in the same direction, or are some oriented the other way? Why? And why are
some seashells found in mountaintops? Are all seashells made
out of the same thing? Does it make a difference if the creatures that live in them come from salt water or fresh water?
There are endless questions. By asking questions and trying to
determine the answers, especially through personal investigation, children find themselves doing science without thinking
it is anything out of the ordinary and gaining, eventually, a
good familiarity with the territory. (24–25)

A confident and interested teacher models those questions and can employ the "lens" of science without becoming a subject specialist. It takes
honesty, enthusiasm, and the ability to search for answers through books
and experiments and experts, but all literacy teachers worth their salt know
how to do that.

Teachers in a science workshop take on two other very important
roles. Aside from helping to identify subjects and activities that profit
from investigation, it is their responsibility to (1) figure out the way the
children in their charge are making sense of what they study and (2) interject
questions that will cause a child to rethink explanations that cannot be
generalized.

Matthew, a second grader, was asked to take a clay ball and "see if
you can find a way to make it float." A casual observer walking into the
room might have seen an intense-looking little boy jabbing his pencil into a
ball of clay, seemingly frustrated and "off-task." His teacher, however,
knew enough to ask this youngster about his activity. "Well," explained
Matthew, "I knew that anyone could float a clay raft, so I decided to make
pumice stone." Sometimes making sense of a child's explanations is simply
a matter of listening. At other points probing questions are needed. A
science workshop is based on the assumption that children are seeking to
make sense, to find consistencies in their world, and to understand what
will enable them to predict and repeat the patterns they see. A large part of
science workshop, then, exists in the mind of the teacher.

But what about children who are obviously "getting it wrong"?
Matthew, for instance, will not be able to create pumice stone out of clay.
It is the teacher's responsibility in these instances to try to create situations

that will worry the child into rethinking the "information" or explanation. Sometimes this is done through an event. Matthew, for instance, might benefit from looking at a piece of pumice stone alongside his clay dotted with holes. In other instances a question might suffice: if he were to report, for instance, that his pumice clay *does* float, the teacher might help the child think through a definition of what it means to float. Do some things float better than others?

Rather than a linear arrangement—starting with subject matter objectives, or developmental theory, or teacher expertise—a workshop focuses on the children's increasing knowledge of the way they learn, are convinced, and convince others. These are the processes teachers and children work together to understand.

Over the years it has become clear to me that many of the children who are "good" in science are those who enjoy the power of being able to name objects or events. Science workshop is designed to invite a different sort of pleasure from studying the natural world; we seek to help children develop a repertoire of strategies for addressing their own curiosities and to recognize, through experience, which questions will be clarified by what activities. Workshop teachers think of science as a lens, a pattern of thought, a conversation that invites even young children to wonder, to speculate, and to satisfy at least some of their curiosities.

If young people leave their elementary schools able to characterize and make explicit what counts as evidence, to generate questions and answers that can be replicated and explained, to face the challenges of science without fear, I suspect that we will have made considerable progress. These goals are those espoused by advocates of large-scale teacher reform, especially those committed to a constructionist approach. What then is the difference between the approach advocated here and the large-scale efforts that seek to effect change?

The Politics of Science Education

In the same way that whole language represents a view of teaching and learning that is at odds with a linear, externally controlled curriculum, science workshop represents a view of the profession as well as a view of teacher education. The intent of scope and sequence charts, lists of "essentials," and other efforts that seek to specify required course content is to make sure that (1) there is a pattern to what children learn and (2) that minimum standards are adhered to. Ideally, such programs ensure that every student is offered an opportunity to engage in worthwhile activities. Although this is certainly a laudable goal, it fosters the notion of minimum competence, both on the part of students and teachers.

To this formulation one must add a general belief among teachers that they know little or nothing about science. If you know nothing, your best bets are to avoid the subject so that your ignorance is less obvious or to use a program that has been so well designed that ignorance is masked. In other words, comprehensive programs, coupled with teachers' insecurities about science, may unwittingly promote disengagement with, distance from, and disinterest in science. Although the comprehensive programs or scope and sequence guides may be useful as a starting point, workshop teachers see their responsibilities as extending far beyond the minimum competence that school systems often establish as a goal.

How do workshop teachers go about expanding their science programs and building on their own professional strengths? Claryce Evans (1990) of the Educator's Forum in Boston notes that, traditionally, practitioners concerned with professional growth move from one in-service program to another learning new information, a new way to use materials, a new way to organize the school day, a new way to deal with parents. It is amazing how little of our professional time is spent reflecting on what we already know, building on what is already working in our classrooms, and giving critical attention to what appears problematic. While other social service professionals such as psychologists and social workers spend hours considering their interactions with their clients, teachers rarely find time to discuss the issues that dominate their thinking about classroom life.

Science workshop makes an explicit attempt to build on the questions, concerns, and support networks that teachers already have in place. Science is not a time to drop all the kid-watching skills we have developed in favor of something new. At this point in history it seems that whole language offers practitioners a matrix of social and political relations as well as an approach to instruction. Workshop teachers can benefit from that whole language community, not only as they think about how children learn to read and write, but also as they consider how children *learn*.

Experienced elementary school teachers often voice their belief that children do not separate the world into discrete branches of knowledge that remain fixed and isolated. As teachers we need to capitalize on intellectual "crossovers," not fight them. The confidence and skill students develop as writers and readers, if encouraged, spill over into science. Reciprocal benefits from science also accrue; the habits of mind students develop as close observers and analytic thinkers serve them well in other academic or social pursuits. The best elementary school teachers seek to foster the wide-ranging interests evidenced by students and celebrate the generalist's urge to make connections in the classroom community.

Sadly, this view of knowledge is not mirrored in the professional opportunities afforded most teachers. To date there is no national organization for educators who wish to learn more about the role of liberal arts education in the elementary schools. In fact, in 1992 at least, the National Council for Teachers of English (NCTE) spring meeting and the National Science Teachers Association (NSTA) annual meeting were scheduled on the same weekend in two different cities. It was impossible for teachers or teacher educators to attend both. Perhaps the alliances among teachers with interests both in whole language and in science teaching need to be forged at the grass roots—initiated by teachers or administrators at the individual school or district level.

The authors of this book are teachers whose classrooms have changed not as the result of a new curriculum package but because of intense professional discussions and extensive reading. They have learned from and with colleagues whose insights and questions made the strange familiar and the familiar strange. They have explored, investigated, and analyzed scientific phenomena themselves so that they could understand what children engaged in science need to think about and feel and understand. The public recital of their own experiences represents a commitment not only to a workshop model but to a profession that values intelligence, community, and caring.

Classroom Views

Although the ideas expressed on the previous pages may appeal to educators, we recognize that ultimately the power of the argument advanced is in its viability as classroom practice. In this sense the heart of *Science Workshop* begins here. Jeanne Reardon's chapter, "Developing a Community of Scientists," offers layers of gifts. For those seeking how-to's this piece is filled with nitty-gritty advice—how to get started, how to arrange materials, how to set up your room. On another level, it is the story of a teacher puzzling out an important problem and sharing many of the questions that have guided her thinking and decisions. The chapter is also a gift because it seeks to demystify what appears as "genius" practice. It tells those seeking how-to's that there are no recipes; entering Jeanne's class next year you will see different practices than you see now. In this sense, the chapter is a tribute to the continuing growth that a life of teaching invites.

In Chapter 3, Anne Schmidt, a teacher in the Baltimore City system, shares not only methods but also her reasons for introducing a science workshop into her classroom in the first place. We are all grateful to Anne, for her articulation of our shared concerns was the impetus for this book. Anne works in a school system generally associated with overcrowding, poverty, and bureaucratic dysfunction. Yet I am struck by the pride both her school and the system have taken in Anne's efforts to expand her curriculum, as well as the support she has received for teacher-initiated change. This chapter gives me hope that other individual teachers might make a difference, both in the lives of children and as leaders in educational reform.

While both Jeanne Reardon and Anne Schmidt came to the science workshop from their experience in and enthusiasm for language teaching, Charles Pearce's commitment to a science workshop springs from his interest in science per se. In his fifth-grade class in a rural Maryland school, one finds children really taking control of the science under consideration and "Mr. Pearce" leading from behind. His notion of the roles and responsibilities of the elementary school science teacher is original and perhaps revolutionary: children design their own questions based on collections of materials he has boxed. His chapter, Chapter 4, reads almost like a paper in progress—I have come this far; we are now in uncharted waters.

Dana Blackwood, a sixth-grade teacher from Fairfax County, Virginia, describes in Chapter 5 how assessment procedures developed for literacy workshops prove useful for students and teachers seeking to evaluate science learning. As a visitor to her classroom, I have learned not only how a master teacher keeps records and follows the progress of the children in her charge, but also how children's own tracking of their progress becomes a central issue in learning. If I were to define a single element as the key to a student's academic success, it would have to do with metacognition, the ability to discern what one knows and doesn't know and how best to go about finding out more. The assessment strategies Dana offers gracefully and modestly teach as well as evaluate.

In a final chapter, Mary Bird, a former science resource teacher in a Boston public school, offers ideas for developing topics that may serve as the basis for workshop learning. Again, this chapter works on at least two levels; it not only presents teachers with excellent, concrete suggestions and materials for getting started with a workshop, but it also proposes a model for creating more workshop topics with children. Don't read this chapter without making a similar list based on a topic for which you feel some deep affection or quirky preoccupation.

This, then, is what the book looks like. We, however, tend to view at it as the beginning of a conversation. Please join us.

References

Evans, C. 1990. Remarks made at the Elementary Science Integration Project Summer Workshop, Baltimore, Md.

Rutherford, J. F. 1991. "Vital connections: Children, books, and science." In *Vital connections: Children, science, and books,* ed. W. Saul and S. Jagusch. Washington, D.C.: Library of Congress. Reprinted by Heinemann Educational Books, Portsmouth, N.H., 1992.

Zubrowski, B. 1990. Remarks made at the Elementary Science Integration Project Summer Workshop, Baltimore, Md.

2 Jeanne Reardon

Developing a Community of Scientists

If you had stopped by our first-grade classroom a year ago and chatted with the children about what they were doing in science, the conversation would have been short, impersonal, and lacking in commitment and detail: "We're studying shadows." "We're watching shadows." "We're drawing shadows." "We're writing about shadows." Occasionally you would have heard the excited voice of a six-year-old scientist, probably male: "I'm watching to see what will happen when I move the light down lower on this box. See, the shadow looks like this when I move it low on the ball, and so . . . "

If you had talked with these same children about what they were doing in reading and writing you would have been showered with a variety of personal and detailed responses:

> I'm reading my last *Curious Dog* book, and I'm thinking about what's going to happen in the next one. I'm calling it *The Curious Dog Returns. . . .*

> Jennifer and I are talking about *Little Raccoon and the Thing in the Pond*. We're trying to figure out if it's the same Lilian Moore who writes the poems. I think it is 'cause she writes like a poet. Listen . . .

> I'm stuck in my writing, so I'm reading for a while. That's what Mrs. Reardon does. It helps her and it helps me.

> Mike's asking me some jokes he's making up for his joke book
> and I'm listening and guessing the answer. Want to try?

> I'm writing a letter to my cousin in India. She sews so I'm telling
> her about the square I made for our Harriet Tubman quilt.

I'm reading . . . thinking . . . talking . . . figuring out . . . stuck . . . asking . . . listening. This talk is familiar to teachers whose children engage in writing workshop. One of the children might have added, "That's what readers and writers do." The children see themselves as readers and writers who engage in the same activities, share the same concerns, struggle with the same problems, and come to understandings in the same way as those in the larger literate community.

I wondered, then, why don't these same children see themselves as scientists? One year later there is a change. We have become scientists. Now you hear:

> I'm pulling water around with this stick and I think the stick
> is like a magnet for water, and then I looked in the hand lens
> at the stick and it's got little hooks, so now I think it's like
> Velcro™, and I'm trying to figure out which it is. Do you think
> it's magnet or Velcro™?"

> I'm watching and looking for changes when I put the water on
> this—it's got oil on it, and this—it's got wax. See the water
> spreads out here, and . . .

> I'm thinking about water, how you can cook it and make steam,
> and then get the water back. . . . That doesn't work for eggs.

> I was reading what I wrote in my journal and I've got all these
> strange things so next I'm going to go back and try . . .

I'm thinking . . . looking for changes . . . that doesn't work . . . so now I think . . . reading what I wrote . . . next I'm. . . . Now "I'm" has replaced "We are." Now you will find it difficult to cut off the rush of conversation—conversation filled with questions and plans for next steps.

In this chapter I tell the story of our change from studying and replicating others' science to working within a community of scientists to construct our own. It is an adventure story—filled with the excitement and tension of exploring the unknown, the anxious moments, and the joyful surprises. As I tell our story I will often share our words. (Frequently I made audiotapes of our meetings so that I could listen to and reflect on our work.) I will also include some of my thinking that led to the decisions made along the way. When I read articles about teachers' practice I am curious about their decisions and find myself asking, What made you decide to do that? What else did you consider? I'll fill you in on my conscious decisions and the way I reached them.

This change in our class grew from my curiosities, questions, and concerns about children's science learning. But it was greatly influenced by my own experiences as a writer and reader, by my experience using a workshop approach in teaching reading and writing, and by my participation as a reading/language arts teacher in the Elementary Science Integration Project (ESIP). I am assuming the reader has experience or familiarity with some form of writing workshop. If you are a teacher whose expertise lies in science and are unfamiliar with writing process and workshop teaching, then some background reading will help you understand my thinking and the comparisons I make. Books by Nancie Atwell (1987), Donald Graves (1983, 1989) and Lucy Calkins (1986) will provide background.

The Story

The story begins with a notation in the spiral notebook I keep of my "Curiosities, Questions, and Concerns": "What is so different about how we are learning science and the way we learn reading and writing?" As I played with this question I thought about the reading and writing community that develops in our classroom each year; I realized we did not have a similar community of scientists. Then came pages of questions. Here are just a few:

What does a scientific community look like? How does it work?

What does a child scientist look like? How does a young child become a scientist? Are there developmental stages most of us go through? Are they the same for the different sciences?

Am I a scientist? How? What do I do that scientists do?

There were also many questions about what scientists do:

How does a scientist solve a problem? What are problems to scientists? How does a scientist decide when a solution is *the* solution?

How does a scientist convince other members of the community to accept an idea or explanation? What is convincing to a scientist?

When do scientists set aside an idea/solution/explanation? What makes them set it aside?

What do scientists do when they get stuck? How do they decide what to do next?

It was about then that Anne Schmidt, a Lucy Calkins disciple and fellow ESIP participant, said, "I think I'll try a science workshop in my classroom." Aha, I thought, maybe that's what holds our writing and reading community together. Maybe a workshop will help build a community of scientists.

Getting Started— A Belly-smacker

In the fall I moved to a new school, Brooke Grove Elementary. It is a suburban school north of Washington, D.C., and a change from the Chapter I schools where I had taught in the past. The community was new to me; I knew none of the children. I wondered if I should wait and establish myself before beginning something new, but quickly decided to go ahead.

Two of the children came to our first-grade classroom able to read a little, and one was familiar with writing workshop from his kindergarten. Soon we were all doing what emerging writers and readers do—struggling to make meaning, sharing our words and illustrations, often delighted, sometimes frustrated. By the end of September our version of reading and writing workshop had taken over the morning and it was time to take the plunge into science workshop. I share that plunge as it happened. (The quotations are unchanged. I have not polished my words, though I was tempted.) It was indeed a plunge, not an Olympic dive, cutting through the water without a ripple. It was more what we called "belly-smackers" when I was a kid. They stung, but the water in the lake felt great.

"What do you think will happen when we have science workshop this afternoon?" I asked the class as we gathered together that Monday morning to go over the plans. "Take a few minutes to think and write down your ideas." I wondered if I was prepared for what would happen next. I began writing. I paused and peeked to see how the children were doing. Most were just sitting (I hoped they were thinking), a few were writing and drawing— after all we had only been in school a few weeks. I wrote some more. "Well, what are you thinking?"

The children began. "It'll be fun." "We'll get to decide what we're going to do." Several children "passed" (that's an option in our discussions). "We'll make potions" (giggles and "yeah"s). "Will you read to us?" "We'll talk." More passes. "We'll write and draw." "We'll make experiments." Finally Matt said, "I don't know what scientists really do, and I don't know what I'll do."

It was then it dawned on me that I didn't know what we were going to do either. Although I had "taught" science for twenty years, had taken science courses in college, and regularly read the science articles in the newspaper, I had not really thought hard about science as a discipline. But I continued:

> We'll be finding out about scientists and what they do. And one way we'll find out what scientists do is by being scientists ourselves. We're finding out about writers by writing, talking about how we write, reading what other writers have written, and thinking about how their writing works. Science workshop will be a little different because . . . because . . . the stuff of science is not words and books. It's . . . other stuff. We just look around and see and read what writers have done. We go to the library or bookstore and get it, but we don't go to the science store, pick out what other scientists have done, and figure out how it works for us. . . . Just like we get to write in writing workshop, we'll get to . . . to . . . "science"—We'll just have to make up new words for what we do. I know some things scientists do and that's where we'll begin this afternoon, but I don't know very much about scientists. It's something I plan to find out.

Since that Monday morning in September I have thought, written, and talked about what that "stuff" of science is. At the moment I believe it isn't the content of the various sciences, it isn't the materials, it isn't symbols and formulas, it isn't inquiry—though that's part of it. I think it is what words are to literature, but I don't yet know what that is for science.

Afternoon came and we had our first science workshop. We met together in a circle on the rug and I explained how we would work:

> For the first few science workshops we'll begin with a mini-lesson about something scientists do when they are doing science. Then we'll do some science using materials and tools of science. We'll have problems to solve just like real scientists, and we'll have a scientists' meeting, like real scientists do. We'll get to write about what we're doing.
>
> Today's minilesson is about observing—observing the same way as scientists. Scientists observe in a way that they can describe *how* they observed and *what* they observed. The *how* is very important to a scientist because some other scientist will want to observe exactly the same way.
>
> First I'll try out some observing with you. I'm going to use this rocking chair. I could look at it and tell you what I *see from where I'm sitting.* That's important to say because it may look quite different from where you sit. Let's try that. . . . Now I could also observe *what happens* when I do this. [I pushed down on the tip of one rocker as I spoke.] Another scientist would want to know more than "I pushed the rocking chair." She'd want to know that I pushed the rocker down with my hand until the very tip touched the rug, then I let it go, and it rocked and it rocked and it rocked slow-er and sl-ow-er until . . . That's what I mean by a scientist's way of observing. It's more than the *what* I saw or heard or felt or smelled—it's the *how* also.
>
> On the circle table you will find some things [four tubs of pattern blocks—flat, wooden blocks of different geometric shapes, each shape a different color—and two tubs of Tinker Toys™] I thought you might want to use to build with while you observe. I bet you can build lots of different things. I will say "stop" every now and then. That means everyone stops and observes. Then we'll share our observations. One other thing—in writing workshop the tables are quiet and the writing talk goes on at the edges of the room. During science workshop this will be reversed: the tables will be for science talk and science work; if you want to work without interruption, you'll need to move to the edges. When I call your name,

pick up some building material and get started. Remember to think about *how* you are observing.

That is how we began. I had put a great deal of thought into selecting this first minilesson. I wanted it to be "real science." I wanted it to be about something critical to science and I chose observation. I wanted this first minilesson to engage the children in an activity that would produce varying accounts so I could better teach the importance of observation. (I would soon discover that every activity resulted in varying accounts.)

I am embarrassed to say my first thought had been to plan a science "exercise." I considered setting out five different materials and having the children observe and describe them. Then the part of me that knows kids and writing said, Why should they observe that stuff? They don't need to look closely at that. It's your need for them to do it. It was then I thought about using construction materials. It was still *my* plan. I knew what I was going to teach them. Fortunately the kids saved me from myself. They began building. As I looked around at their growing constructions, I picked up a small block and began to wonder. What was I doing? I was about to build their science out of small blocks, one piece at a time. We didn't write and read by having me pass out one word at a time, and I realized that we wouldn't build our community of scientists that way either.

I moved in to watch their construction. I saw boys with all of the Tinker Toys™, girls with the pattern blocks, boys building up and girls building flat. One of the girls went over to get some Tinker Toys™ and was told, "You don't know how to use these." The maleness and the exclusionary nature of science came flooding back to me. My journal from that day contains comments and questions:

> How did it happen that you had to already be good at science, to have proof and the right answers, *before* you were allowed into the club? Where did the authority of science come from? . . . "Don't come in unless you have all of the facts, and you can't get the facts unless you are in." Six years old and already . . . What's going on here? It's no wonder so little science learning goes on in classrooms—so few elementary teachers ever were admitted to the club. Is it something inherent in science—cold, hard, objectivity without emotion—is that what science is really like? . . . It's going to be different in our room. We're really going to build a community—and it's going to include the girls!

Now, with a year and a half of science watching behind me, I would stay with the kids' buildings, discuss the gender issue, attend to their science, and extend it. We would become engineering scientists. But this was September and I was still taking belly-smackers. I watched that first afternoon, handled the gender comments, then gave them a new observation problem the next day. (You take a belly-smacker because you're afraid to go in headfirst, so the last moment you pull your head up, and then—smack.)

Going in Headfirst

It was a hot October day, we had just returned from PE, and I had begun reading *Frederick* by Leo Lionni (1967) when we were startled by rain pounding against the windows. I thought for a moment it was hail; it certainly was a sound that demanded our attention. I suggested we move to the windows to find out what was happening. We looked. The kids were riveted to the windows, and as we all watched the rain I thought, This is it! This is the catalyst to set off a real scientific exploration. Sound, light, color, reflections, weather, drops . . . What shall we focus on? What are the kids ready for? What can they do now? Where is their interest?

I remembered Bernie Zubrowski, an author and scientist from the Boston Museum of Science who had worked with our Elementary Science Integration Project over the summer. Bernie had said certain materials are intrinsically interesting. Water fit! I saw myself as a child standing by a window watching and wondering: Which drop will let go first? When those two bump what will happen? Which will win the race to the bottom? Drops are pretty interesting, they move, they're easy to make, and watch, and manipulate; they change. And, I later discovered, girls come into science on the same footing as boys when the material is water. I said to the class, "Look at the glass; don't look through it."

After watching another five minutes we met back on the rug to talk about what we noticed. "Big drops go faster." "No, some big drops don't go at all." "Little drops go fast when they hit a trail—then they zoom right on down." "I didn't see that." "Let's go back and look." So we went back to observe some more, but the rain had gone as quickly as it had come: "The drops are disappearing!" We met again on the rug. I knew the problem we would work on for our next science workshop. I asked, "How can we study and find out more about those raindrops *inside* our classroom? What if a scientist wanted to find out more about rain drops falling on the window; would she have to wait until the next rain? Be thinking about this for tomorrow's workshop."

Our next workshop began with a "quick write" in response to our problem: How can we find out more about rain drops inside our room? Some children wrote, others drew experimental designs. Everyone had an idea as we worked on a problem common to other scientists, how to replicate natural phenomena in a laboratory setting. Valita even wondered if the drops would be the same when we brought them inside. We talked about laboratory study and field study. I wondered with the kids if studying living organisms changes them. We met safety concerns when we talked about using glass. This moved us into a discussion of materials we would use in our room. An hour had passed and we were still on the rug working out our plans.

You might be surprised that a verbal science exploration could hold six-year-olds' attention for that amount of time. I think it is an indication that we were exploring a problem that was important to us.

As I look back, this was the day we began to build a community of scientists. We had a real problem that we needed to solve before we could go on. It was ours, unique in the sense that no one had ever met and solved this exact problem before. Others have investigated drops of water, but no one had brought the problem into our classroom. It was up to us to figure out how to bring those drops in and find out how they worked. I am not suggesting that it is never appropriate to see what others have done, to see how they may have approached your problem. But I believe that if emerging scientists are going to experience science in a way that will lead them to understand the processes of science, we need to give them opportunities to look to themselves and their classmates as problem solvers and science authorities.

We decided that we would need a substitute for glass, and noted that we had plenty of water at the sink. The kids would bring in materials that water would run off or drop on. Making the drops would be our problem for the next workshop. I brought in several pieces of Plexiglas™, and set out a stack of Styrofoam™ lunch trays, newspapers, and plastic cups for water. (Our school lunches are served on Styrofoam™ trays similar to those used in the meat department at grocery stores. The used trays are sent out for recycling, but are also available for classroom use.) I also made Popsicle™ sticks and drinking straws available as alternatives to fingers for "drop making."

Before the next workshop I explored drops myself using these materials. I did some thinking about:

- Organization of materials and setup and cleanup procedures.
- Kids' writing and record keeping (logs, paper, format, time for writing, possible prompts).

- My record keeping (tapes, notes, status-of-class-forms).
- Scientists' meeting arrangements (where, when, procedures, record keeping for meeting).
- Possible minilessons.

This became the list I regularly used as I went over what had happened, and prepared for the next workshop. Some of the items became routine (organization of materials, cleanup procedures, my record keeping on self-stick notes, status-of-the-class notes). We always included a scientists' meeting in our workshops, but the purpose and structure varied.

The next afternoon's plans read, "After music we'll have science workshop; we'll explore making water drops." The class had me insert "YEAH!!" after science workshop. We could hardly wait. We started with a short minilesson covering procedures for getting materials, then the exploration began. I stopped by the tables, watched, and chatted: "How's it going? . . . What are you doing? . . . What's happening? . . . What do you notice? After fifteen minutes I had the children stop, passed out blank journals, and asked the kids to write about what they had done, then to continue exploring. Most of the kids lay on the floor and wrote for about fifteen minutes, then went back to the tables. After ten minutes more I had the class stop to clean up, and then bring their journals and a pencil up to the rug for a scientists' meeting.

Scientists' Meetings

I introduced the meeting by saying:

> One way scientists find out what other scientists are working on and thinking about is by reading. Scientists write a lot so there's lots to read. They write for magazines and journals, they write reports and letters. Of course they talk to each other too. Another way they find out is by going to meetings. Sometimes the meetings are small with just a few scientists who are working on the same kinds of things; sometimes there are big meetings of scientists from many countries. One or two scientists will report their work to a group and the rest will listen, ask questions, talk, and argue about the ideas they hear.
>
> Usually we'll have one or two of the scientists in our room discuss their work, but today we'll all talk around the circle

and I'll be the recorder. First I want you to think about something you *did*, or something you *observed* or *noticed*, or something you *wonder about*. You may want to read what you wrote in your journal to help you remember. After you decide what you are going to share, write a "D" if it is something you did, an "O" if it's something you observed or noticed, and a "W" if it's something you wonder about. Then put your journal and pencil down and get ready to listen to the other scientists.

When we share all around the circle it is important for each initial contribution to be short and focused. This technique helps the children pick out one thing to tell. The following list brought us partway around:

- "I used my fingers to make drops and the water hung on and wouldn't let go."
- "I made puddles."
- "I cut my drop in two with the Popsicle™ stick."
- "You can pull water around with a stick. It just follows the stick."
- "I can pick up water with a straw and let it go in big drops."
- "Some drops are taller than others."
- "Drops fall 'cause they're heavy."
- "I had drop races."
- "You can blow drops all around and make them bump into other drops until they get so big they aren't drops."
- "Drops jiggle."
- "Drops are hard to see. It'd be easier if we colored them."
- "I put foil on my tray and they went faster."
- "When I put a stick in my cup it looks sort of broke. I took it out and it's not. I put it back and it's broke again."
- "Just before drops fall they change shape."

I recorded everything, writing the child's initials by the contribution, then read over the list of observations, activities, suggestions, and explanations. (You notice that not all of the comments fit my categories. Some children regularly give explanations while observing—drops fall because they're heavy, water follows the stick. I came to see these as responses to the child's questions, and we would work to uncover the questions which lay behind the explanations.) Next I directed the children to draw a line across their journal page and below the line to add anything they wanted to try for themselves, find out more about, or talk over with someone. I suggested they write the name of the person who had done the work so that they could get together. Then I had each child tell me his or her plan for the next workshop. (In writing workshop I record plans at the end of workshop on my status-of-the-class sheet [Atwell 1987]. I find that it helps first graders to make plans at the end of session. I read this list for confirmation. I might ask, You're continuing with your joke book, right? before the kids begin work the next time. I followed this same practice in science workshop.)

As the year went on I found our scientists' meetings critical to the construction of science knowledge and to an understanding of the ways of science. They provided time for essential information exchange. Of greater importance, it was during meetings that we were confronted with alternative observations, findings, and explanations—and expected to decide which were convincing. We sometimes found it difficult to support or revise our own findings and explanations. I continued to use minilessons to expose children to pieces of science, but they were a minor part of our workshop. The challenge of science came in our meetings.

In meetings the children were very accepting of each other's findings, but at the same time they wanted to try things out and see for themselves. After we began using water colored with food coloring to make our drops, color became an important factor. "Red drops go faster than yellow ones." "I split my green drop and got little blue drops out of it." (Now that's pretty interesting.) Several children would ask more about such observations so they could try the same thing. The need for demonstrations became apparent and so we began to schedule demonstrations as part of our scientists' meetings. At this time I introduced replicability as an important scientific practice. While the ability to replicate became important to many children, there was still widespread belief in and acceptance of the one-time occurrence.

About once a week the meeting focused on a problem springing from something I had noticed during hands-on work time, or something said during a meeting. It might be a problem that would extend children's understanding of how scientists work. I would pose the problem in both a general and specific form. These problem-solving meetings usually came at the beginning of workshop before hands-on time.

Today in our meeting we are going to think about what kind of evidence convinces us that an explanation really explains what is happening. Yesterday Mike reported he could push water through wood. He said that he had two Popsicle™ sticks and when he pushed down on the top stick he could push water right through the bottom one. Mike told us how he knew—what evidence he had. Remind us how you knew, Mike.

"I felt under the bottom stick and it was wet, and I'd been pushing down on it."

I want you to write down or draw pictures of a test you could use to convince yourself that Mike's explanation, pushing down, really explains the water under the stick. Then we'll share our tests and try them out.

Designing tests was difficult for children the entire year. Most of the children saw explanations as evidence. They saw no need for tests. "There's a hole in the stick, that's how the water gets there" became a "test." Valita was the first, and one of the few, to isolate and control variables when designing tests. "First you have to make sure your hands are dry and the sticks are dry. Then you put the top stick in water and press it down hard on the other stick. You get someone else with dry hands to feel if the water went through." I do not teach lessons on variables, but let them emerge or develop from the need to communicate and convince others. Then afterwards I explain that this is one of the ways scientists work; it is a convention of science work, just as punctuation is a convention of writing. (Communication in science calls for a different kind of logic from that of poetry. We expect poets to think and write in metaphors, but would be uncomfortable if a scientist told us, "The rain, they say, is a mouse gray horse . . .' [Bennett 1937].)

Hands-on Explorations and Investigations

Hands-on science is seen as essential to science learning, and I have said little about the hands-on part of our workshops. I mentioned briefly the afternoon when we began making drops. The children got their materials and you heard me asking, How's it going? What's happening? What are you doing? What do you notice?

That is what we call exploration. We may have a general sort of problem, but no real question, no explanation we're trying to test. It's just a getting-to-know-the-possibilities time, a messing-about time—*a very important time.* This is where data come from. This is when patterns emerge, predictions are made, questions and explanations spring up. Some children stay with exploration during most of the hands-on time. Some have no direction and shop around for ideas of ways to interact with the materials. There is a lot of borrowing and trying out, as well as just plain random messing about.

For most children investigations grow out of explorations. In our room we distinguish between explorations and investigations. Investigations are directed and purposeful explorations. They come in response to a hunch, a question, an idea. This is a trying-out time. It is a time when concepts are constructed. Children move in and out of explorations and investigations during hands-on time. There may be a lot of talk, or there may be quiet concentration. I watch, confer, listen and ask questions. This is rather similar to the role I take in writing and reading conferences. I do a lot of "playing back" (Giacobbe 1986). When given explanations, I often ask, How do you know? I find that the move from *what* to *how* is a difficult transition. Some children stay at the "what happened" stage for months; others move through "what I did" to "how I did that" to "how I know."

You have noticed that the children choose how and when to explore and decide on their investigations, but I set the topic—I was the one who chose water drops. (After french toast and syrup appeared on the lunch menu, it became imperative to study syrup drops; at that point we moved into other liquids.) There was a period of time when we worked on "liquid-proofing" different fabrics. We spent six months on liquid-related study. At the end of the year we dealt with the school system's required curriculum topics—shadows, plants, and aquariums—using the same workshop framework.

I think about removing this topic restriction and having the children select their own topics just as we do in writing. I ask myself why I haven't, and I have a couple of explanations. Science materials are not accessible in the way that materials for reading and writing are. We have thousands of books available in the media center and libraries, easy access to paper, pencils, and markers. But I think the real explanation is that I'm afraid— I'm afraid I don't know enough science, and I don't know myself well enough as a scientist to pose the questions that will extend the children's scientific understandings.

I don't need to read a book in order to discuss it with another reader; in fact, sometimes it is more fun to talk about books I haven't read. I do think I am better able to help a reader or writer because I have read widely and written in the genre being used. In a sense I have constructed my own knowledge through my reading and writing experiences. (Most of my science knowledge is secondhand, book knowledge, not of my making.) Readers construct personal meaning from the written text whether it is fiction or nonfiction. Readers assimilate only as much as they are able to use at the time. Sometimes a reader does not understand, or misunderstands. One could argue, *That* is not what the author said. Your meaning is not valid. Through discussion, other readers in the class and I can make available alternative understandings. In the case of nonfiction, some understandings are clearly more accurate than others. Some readers' understandings are *not* valid.

I would say that is also the case in science. Using observations and data, together with other knowledge and experience, the scientist (child or credentialed adult) constructs explanations. Some are more accurate than others. Some are not valid. Then why does it become a problem for me in science and not in reading? The difficulty is that I am unable to suggest alternate explanations if my own and the other class members' conceptual understanding is limited or inaccurate. While I have an understanding of many basic concepts, science is very specialized and I find it easier to read up on and play with one limited area at a time. So for now I shall set the general field of study.

Writing During Science Workshop

It is difficult to imagine a science workshop without writing—we wrote during every workshop. The workshop writing was all single-draft, personal writing. It worked for us in different ways: "quick writes" focused our thinking before we discussed; our problem-solving and planning writing was usually in narrative form; we kept records and made drawings of observations; and we reflected on our observations in our journals. We did not do any formal report writing during science workshop, although some children chose to write on science topics during morning writing workshop.

During hands-on exploration and investigation time, the children recorded whatever was important to them in any form they chose. Mini-lessons exposed the class to a variety of formats used by scientists, but most children chose to write narratives. I tried having the children record results in chart form as a way to keep track of their explorations and investigations as they worked to waterproof fabric. I watched as some children struggled to fill in the charts we had developed together and written on the chalkboard. In truth these charts were not helpful to them. Finally Chris said to me, "I'm going to write in my way and if you want a chart we can make it in meeting." And so I made the announcement the class had heard in other ways before, "Stop just a minute. Chris has told me this chart making is not helping him and I wonder if it's helping you. Just go back to writing the way that works for you. We'll talk about it later."

Writing done during the hands-on time provides data, but not in the form I typically associate with science. (My idea of typical science data comes from the records I kept in labs—lots of numbers and precise drawings.) The kids' data look more like the ethnographic data of my own classroom research. Precise, quantitative data are needed when measuring change, but one does not need the same quantitative data to notice patterns, build explanations, and recognize change. One needs experience in reading and looking. Frequently I used children's writing to demonstrate how to read for patterns, or read to detect change. Donald Graves (1989) notes, "Understanding change is what literacy is all about. Drawing, recording, and reflecting on the sequences of activities help us to see differently" (26). I would argue that seeing differently and understanding change are also what science is about.

We wrote during scientists' meetings as well as during hands-on time. During meetings children wrote responses to my questions, questions chosen to push their thinking in different directions and to let me in on the content and strategies of their thinking about science. Their responses provide the data I use to plan my next steps. These are not easy questions. It is very quiet as we struggle to find and write our response. These young children do not write at length, but I believe strongly in the power of writing to form ideas, and so we write. Some of the questions we responded to during the year are:

- What have you discovered?
- How do you know?
- What do you wonder?
- What will you do next? How do you decide what to do next?
- How do you decide what to record?
- How do you use your log?
- What helps you do science?
- What are you doing when you do science?
- How do you know when to stop, that you are finished?

• Do you ever give up (abandon) your idea/question/explanation? Why? When?
• What makes you revise your explanation?

Sharing our responses makes available the thinking of our fellow scientists and gives us new ways of thinking and working.

Reading and Science

If you entered our classroom before the children arrived, the dominant impression you would receive would be books. There are revolving racks of books; shelves of books; author, poetry, and thematic displays; writing resource books; and the books included with art, music, mathematics, and science center materials. We always have fiction, exposition, reference books, poetry, magazine articles, and art prints alongside science materials at the science center. And how are these "science" books used by the children?

Science books are read, discussed, and checked out daily, but very rarely does a child pick up a book during science workshop: books that were in such initial demand that a sign-up list had to be written on the chalkboard sit untouched.

At first I was surprised that children who are active, critical readers do not use books during science workshop. I remembered other years when similar books were read during science time. We talked about this one day. I told the class what I had noticed, that they frequently read and shared science books during reading workshop and took them home to read, but did not pick them up during science workshop. They seemed amazed that anyone would think about reading during science workshop. After one child asked me if I ever thought about reading then, I asked why it seemed such a strange idea; weren't they curious about how other scientists thought or what was known about the science they were doing?

It seems that books are not relevant to the science being practiced by these children during workshop time. ("You don't need books for what you can find out." "I don't need a book to tell me. I know.") Science is very personal, and questions demand immediate attention from these six-year-olds. This is a time to see and do, a time for acting, not reading about the findings of others. They move quickly between exploring, wondering, investigating their questions, wondering, playing, wondering, explaining. The children's comments about science throughout this chapter are indicative of their personal involvement and confidence in their findings. At this age they do not look to others or to books for confirmation of their findings. Perhaps the reason children read science books during science other years was because the problems they were working on came from outside them—from me or from question cards. The children involved in science workshop are working with their own problems, and they rely on themselves to discover solutions.

It is difficult for young children to slow down to reflect and reconsider while they are exploring and investigating. This is the reason writing and scientists' meetings are so important to the workshop. The writing, discussions, and demonstrations provide time to slow down and think about what individual scientists see, and how they explain.

Although books are not needed or used by these children during the workshop time, they are an important part of their science thinking and learning. Just as writing and science meetings provide time, the science books that the children read during reading workshop also create time for the child. A child reading a book has time to stop and wonder about science, to imagine, to ask questions, to put self into the picture, to make connections to the world, to gaze off into space and think, to go back and reconsider, and to play with ideas.

Frequently I read science books aloud to the class, books that are invitations to explore the strange as well as the familiar, science adventure stories, science mysteries, information books. (See Reardon 1991 for a more detailed description of the roles of science books in the classroom.)

I have noticed that since we have been engaged in science workshop the children read in a new way; they read with a scientist's eye. There is a greater attention to detail in illustrations portraying the natural world. I hear comments about how much of Boris (Steig 1971) is under water and how close he could get to land without hitting the bottom. The children expect scientific accuracy in the illustrations of books that describe real behavior of animals. They notice when caterpillars have furry antennas, smile, and spin cocoons.

Conclusion

This chapter tells the story of children learning science by becoming members of an active community of scientists, by doing what scientists do. The children's hands-on exploration and investigation play an important part in their science learning. Fortunately hands-on science experience is integral to science programs in many classrooms. However our hands-on experiences alone did not develop the community or our sense of science. I believe the children's writing and participation in scientists' meetings, as well as my close listening, questioning, analysis, and planning, were crucial to the development of our community. Whether we call this interaction of hands-on exploration and investigation, writing, and meeting "science workshop" is not important. What is important is the development of the classroom community of scientists that brings us into the larger community of scientists.

Concluding this chapter is both difficult and easy. It is difficult because I have much more to write about how we worked and what the children and I learned about science, scientists, and science learning. I want to tell you about reading science, the content of our writing, about the children's science explanations, about how "borrowing" worked in our community, about science language and how it changed . . . and so it is difficult to stop writing.

It is easy to stop because you who are teachers will continue writing this story. This is the beginning, and the story will grow and change each year as we watch and learn from children who are permitted to become scientists. Writing our science workshop stories and descriptions will provide the data we need to develop our own theory and guide us in our change.

References

Atwell, N. 1987. *In the middle: Writing, reading, and learning with adolescents*. Portsmouth, N.H.: Boynton/Cook.

Bennett, R. B. 1937. "Rain." In *Under the tent of the sky,* comp. by J. W. Brewton. New York: Macmillan.

Calkins, L. M. 1986. *The art of teaching writing*. Portsmouth, N.H.: Heinemann.

Giacobbe, M. E. 1986. A writer reads, a reader writes. In *Understanding writing: Ways of observing, learning and teaching,* ed. by T. Newkirk and N. Atwell. Portsmouth, N.H.: Heinemann.

Graves, D. H. 1983. *Writing: Teachers and children at work*. Portsmouth, N.H.: Heinemann.

———. 1989. *Investigate nonfiction. The reading/writing teacher's companion.* Portsmouth, N.H.: Heinemann.

Lionni, L. 1967. *Frederick.* New York: Pantheon.

Moore, L. 1963. *Little raccoon and the thing in the pond.* New York: McGraw Hill.

Reardon, S. J. 1991. Children, science, and . . . books? A teacher explains. In *Vital connections: Children, science, and books,* ed. by W. Saul and S. Jagusch. Washington, D.C.: Library of Congress. Reprinted by Heinemann Educational Books, Portsmouth, N.H., 1992.

Steig, W. 1971. *Amos and Boris.* New York: Farrar, Straus, and Giroux.

3 Anne Schmidt

"When Lava Lets Loose": A Science Workshop Heats Up

For the past twenty-some years I have been doing science the same way, the way we had learned it in our college courses. I began with a motivating activity, the big splash, for which I would gather visuals, design a new bulletin board, check out books from the library, and locate a decent film-strip. This required significant thought and preparation time and, frankly, I learned a lot in the process. Although in writers' workshop we approached the process of learning in an entirely different manner, it never occurred to me that *science* could allow for the same student involvement and control and initiative that characterizes our writing workshop.

What finally drove me from this teacher-controlled science instruc-tion was the clear vision of the way children in my class took to writers' workshop. There were two major successes here. The first had to do with content. We, the children and I, were impressed that each and every one of us became writers; we had something to say and were able to get our ideas onto paper in a way that made sense to readers. And second, there was no feeling that these kids were doing a painful assignment. They treated their work seriously; their pieces were their own and they evidenced a pride about their work that was rarely seen in anything else they did in or out of school.

When I had first heard about a writers' workshop I was skeptical about its chances for success, mainly because of the type of school environ-ment in which the children and I work. My class is in a typically urban school. Many of the students come from low-income or single-parent families. There are thirty-four students in a relatively small classroom stuffed to the gills with plants, books, kids' papers, and other collectibles. It's a Chapter I school and my class population is 100 percent minority. Although we have enough basal readers for every child in the class, other supplies, like paper and reference and trade books, are severely limited. Science materials, to date, have been virtually nonexistent.

Was it possible, I thought, for me to give up control in science as I had in writers' workshop? Would the same kind of involvement be evident in a science workshop that we had seen in our writers' workshop? Several years ago, I spent my time correcting every student paper, filling in words, circling misspelled ones, underlining capitalization and punctuation errors. What enabled me to give that up? It wasn't easy—paper correcting can become a way of life—and I felt insecure about allowing children, even second graders, to go home with work that looked less than perfect.

My change had been less a matter of philosophical commitment than a result of my curiosity about whether this workshop model could actually succeed in my classroom. But it had. Children became involved in and committed to their ideas in a way I had never dreamed possible. And because they were able to develop their own stories and poems and arguments, they became more invested in their own writing and more interested in issues of revision and correctness. It was no longer a matter of doing these things for Ms. Schmidt but for themselves. Would this same approach invite children to become serious investigators and owners of their work in science?

The Minilesson

I knew that I needed some sort of organizational structure for a science workshop. Since my students were already very familiar with the structure of our writers' workshop, I decided to adopt something similar.

We would begin each workshop hour with a brief minilesson. Since we like to move around in our classroom, I would call the children to the back of the room. There all thirty-five of us would huddle up as a group and wait to begin.

Our first minilesson was basically just a question. I wanted to start somewhere. Our topic was earth science, and I really didn't know what background knowledge the children had. So I brought in a coconut still in its outer shell and asked, What is this? I expected to get a few responses and then an answer. This would lead us into further investigations of the earth and its resources. But what I got from my class completely surprised me.

What was supposed to be a brief introduction turned into an hour-long discussion during which I contributed very little. One student would ask a question about the object and someone else would respond. After a while, I was able to sit and listen, reflect, and take notes on a conversation among thirty-four kids who had a surprising amount of knowledge, even if they had no experience with coconuts or the tropics.

This was really exciting. For the most part, students had been totally involved in the lesson, and had demonstrated what the college texts call higher-level thinking skills: drawing their own conclusions, making judgments, and supporting opinions with observable data.

From this first lesson, I realized that I needed to make each mini-lesson simple and straightforward, focusing on one particular skill or activity at a time. We used the minilesson to do everything from develop a list of guidelines on behavioral expectations for group work to demonstrate a piece of science equipment.

Many of my most successful lessons included the sharing of literature or a science trade book. When I shared Joanna Cole's *The Magic School Bus Inside the Earth* (1987), for instance, my purpose was to focus attention on our topic, volcanos, but also to build a basic background of information. Not only did the story grab everyone's attention, it generated a fact list on volcanos that took two boards to contain. As we were looking over our list, one student commented: "I didn't know I knew so much about the earth and volcanos!" After this lesson, the students couldn't wait to get to work on their own research on volcanos.

By browsing through the public libraries, I found a wealth of excellent children's literature that could be used to support our required topics. Most of my preparation time for the minilessons was spent on the floor of the library, sitting cross-legged, reading children's books. And in the classroom, we kept our science workshop books on a special cart where they were always available. These books were usually the first ones selected during the silent reading time.

Some minilessons were much more mundane. From time to time, I found it necessary to review in-house matters such as the passing out and collecting of science materials. One minilesson was devoted to sharing ideas on how best to work with water in a crowded classroom. (The class and I found that no matter how careful everyone was, water still found its way to the floor, sometimes a bucketful at a time!)

Keeping each lesson brief was often difficult, but I discovered that the more I tried to cover in one lesson, the less successful the lesson would be. At the end of each science workshop, I spent a minute evaluating what had happened that day. This often helped to give me the topic for the next day's minilesson. For example, one lesson involved designing a chart to organize the results of the previous day's investigation into different types of rocks the students had collected. The directions had been to develop a chart of one's own design on which to record the observations of the rocks. When I saw that most of my students were having difficulty not with the observations but with designing an organizational strategy for charting clearly, I knew what my next minilesson would be. The next day, the class brainstormed a list of ideas for designs that they thought would clearly display observable data about rocks. This done, the students were able to select from the list of ideas for charts and design a clear and understandable chart of their own.

Investigation Time

Although minilessons are important and the particular responsibility of the teacher, the heart of the workshop is the children's investigation time—their time to explore and wonder and worry ideas into place. The involvement that I sought to foster I knew was an outgrowth of the students' taking chances, making decisions, and putting their ideas together to make a kind of personal sense.

During the investigation time, children were involved with a variety of activities: exploring materials, working through either suggested or self-initiated experiments, researching topics of scientific interest, talking through problems with their peers, and communicating responses or results.

DeWayne decided to investigate characteristics of water, and I worried some about the amount of time he spent at the sink. Using graduated measuring containers, he would carefully fill a liter tin can, then pour its contents into a smaller vessel, making comparisons over and over. This was his own idea and he proceeded with little or no teacher direction. I was also fascinated by his involvement and the care with which he measured. Several weeks later, when we began our study of metric equivalencies, DeWayne was a self-taught expert.

Experiments were also popular and profitable activities for investigation time. During our study of air, one group in particular impressed me with its ability to think through a problem. The children were investigating properties of air, so they set up two experiments on air that they had found in a classroom reference. One of the experiments was to blow on a single sheet of paper placed across two books spaced several inches apart. The other experiment was to hold two sheets of paper parallel to each other and blow between them. In both cases, the paper does the opposite of what we first expect. In the first case, the paper goes down instead of being blown away (see Figure 3–1). In the second, the two sheets move together instead of being blown apart (see Figure 3–2).

The results of the experiments certainly surprised the group, and the students began to hypothesize about the reasons for those results. For each experiment, the group came up with what seemed to them a reasonable explanation for the results they had obtained. When I questioned them, they were able to explain their conclusions with a great deal of logic. They asserted that the results of the first experiment were caused by there being

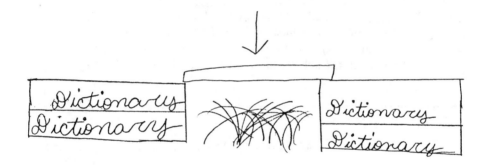

FIGURE 3–1. Experiment one on the properties of air.

more air over the paper than under it. In the second experiment, they concluded that the air was stronger than the paper, and thus the papers were forced together.

This group had selected a topic to explore, found ways to test the topic, and formulated some theories that were reasonable to the group members.

My first obligation as a workshop teacher was to congratulate them on their hard thinking. A second and important response was to play the always skeptical scientist. Could they come up with another experiment that would prove their theory about the weight of air?

Some topics are conducive more to research in books than to hands-on experimentation. I was continually surprised by the children's enthusiasm for this research work, especially when I thought back to my own experiences as a child. Perhaps this enthusiasm was the result of the research questions posed—they were generated and chosen by the children themselves. Perhaps it had something to do with the variety of materials that were made available. My usual tactic was to raid the library and bring in any and all books on the subject at hand. For children who had few books

FIGURE 3–2. Experiment two on the properties of air.

available this felt a little like Christmas. Their excitement may also have had something to do with the social nature of the research. Some worked in pairs of their own choosing; others worked by themselves, eager to see their ideas displayed as a grand individual effort, to know that what was produced was theirs and theirs alone.

Davon, a recent transfer from another school, systematically pursued the topic of volcanos. His research was especially exhilarating for me to watch develop. Although the reading was difficult for him because of the advanced reading level of the books he had selected, he consistently used the skills at his disposal to figure out unknown words. And even though many other children in the class could use standard spelling and punctuation more effectively and volunteered to help, he was emphatic about making this piece his own. When he had finished his research and written his report, he couldn't wait to share what he had done. That moment was one of my most satisfying as a teacher. I'll never forget the look of pride and happiness on his face as he shared his piece (Figure 3–3) with the class:

Volcanos

Volcanos have something that is called magma. Before it is lava, it is magma, and lava is made up of hard melted rock.

When volcanos erupt, they erupt with a loud boom, and when lava lets loose, whatever is in the path that the lava is moving, it burns up. And when the lava cools off, it is hard rock with a shiny coat.

Talking through a problem with group members also played an important part in our investigation time. Because of the size of the class and limitations of space as well as materials, we did much of our experimenting in groups of two or more. This made it necessary for the kids working together to come to group decisions. Agreeing on solutions wasn't always easy, but it was always interesting. One pair of boys decided to settle an argument on how to draw Jupiter by slugging it out on the playground. A reminder that they were really good friends quickly restored order. They began to talk together and after only a short time came to the agreement that Henry would draw Jupiter because he was better at art stuff, and Will would label the picture because he was the better writer.

As I walked around the room during investigation time observing groups working, I was delighted to hear several budding scientists intensely discussing conclusions they could draw from their experiment on

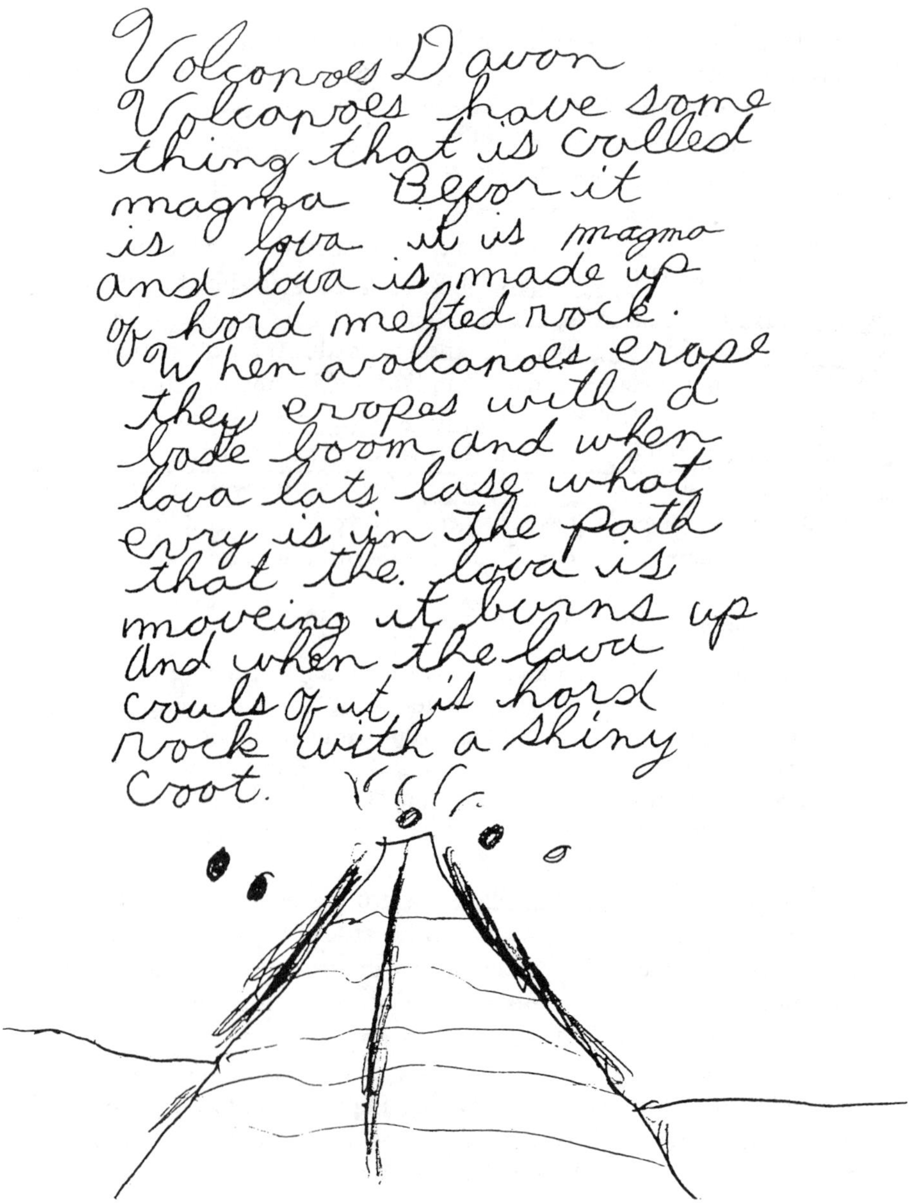

Volcanoes D avon

Volcanoes have some
thing that is called
magma Befor it
is lava it is magma
and lava is made up
of hard melted rock.
When a volcanoes erope
they eropes with a
lode boom and when
lova lats lase what
evry is in the path
that the. lova is
moveing it burns up
and when the lava
couls of ut, it hard
rock with a shiny
coot.

FIGURE 3–3. Davon's piece on volcanos.

condensation; another group huddled together sharing theories on why the paper towel in the overturned glass held under water didn't get wet. It was up to me to ask each child to support the theory. Usually I would ask the group to explain how they had come to an agreement, or how they had solved their problem. I could not only get an idea of how they were thinking, I could also use their responses as informal assessment.

How to communicate the results of the experiments and research was also decided during the investigation time. Three different groups of students investigating the sunflower arrived at three different ways to communicate their findings to the class. One group created a booklet containing text and pictures of the sunflower. A second group decided to build a life-size model of the sunflower and give an oral description as they displayed their model. The third group chose a written report accompanied by a labeled diagram. As I watched these students preparing their research for presentation, it was evident that they were having a great time working, researching, making decisions, and communicating. Playing the investigator myself, I asked each group in turn to formulate a statement about why they had decided to present their findings in the particular way they'd chosen. The booklet group agreed that they did a book because they loved reading books and felt comfortable working in that format. The model group said that they really enjoyed working with art materials and couldn't wait to get into our colored-paper drawer. The group that presented a written report and diagram had gotten the idea from looking at diagrams of sunflowers in an old encyclopedia.

Communicating research and results turned out to be very much a decision-making activity. As I read Tiffany's piece on volcanos (Figure 3–4), I was fascinated by the way she wrote her report.

Volcanos

When volcanos get mad they do terrible things. Let me tell you about it. Well, when a volcano erupts that means it's mad. It spits out steam and the steam is turned into rain. It may mix with dust, ashes, and splatter to the ground in torrents of mud. Then magma in the volcano comes out because the volcano's very mad. Magma is lava. It has killed many people, animals, and land. Even plants die. The lava solidifies and then lava has a new name, *lapilli*. Then clouds of gas are spit into the air. After the volcano gets all of its anger out of its system it is as calm as the sea.

> ### Volcanoes
>
> When volcanoes get mad they do terrible things. Let me tell you about it. Well, when a volcanoe erupts that means it's mad. It spits out steam and the the steam is turned into rain. It may mix with dust, ashes, and splatter to the ground in torrents of mud. Then magma in the volcanoe comes out because the volcanoe's very mad. Magma is lava. It has killed many people, animals, and land. Even plants die. The lava soldifys and then lava has a new name Lapilli. Then clouds of gas is spit into the air. After the volcanoe gets all of it's anger out of it's system it is as calm as the sea.
>
> Tiffany Parson

FIGURE 3–4. Tiffany's piece on volcanos.

My curiosity aroused, I asked Tiffany why she had made her volcano seem to take on human characteristics. I thought she might not be sure of the difference between fantasy and reality. But I needn't have worried. She replied that she had used personification (her word!) to make her report more interesting. (We had studied personification often in writers' workshop.) She also said that her idea of giving a volcano human characteristics had come from a TV documentary. There was certainly some decision making going on here.

Student decision making happens over and over again during the investigation time. This list suggests but a few of the decisions class members made:

- How do you set up an investigatory activity so that a specific question can be answered?
- What kinds of research materials do you need to find answers to specific questions?
- What (if anything) do the results of your experiment lead you to conclude?
- How can you best communicate your research or results to the class?
- Which group member will be best suited for each task?
- Which question(s) do you or your group wish to work on?
- What kind of collection will you be working on?
- What strengths does each group member have that the group can capitalize on?
- What other experiments can be done to test your theory?
- Are your results or conclusions logical?
- How can you most accurately measure your results?
- How can our group come to some sort of agreement?

Here's a list of materials I kept on hand for use during classroom investigation:

- A set of graduated liquid and solid measures.
- Plastic bowls and dishpans of various sizes.
- Plastic spoons.
- Straws.
- A plastic or metal pitcher.
- Paper cups.
- String.
- Yardsticks.
- Paper towels.
- Salt.
- Sugar.
- Vinegar.
- Plastic zip-lock bags.

- Various-size boxes for collections.
- Food coloring.
- Tape.
- Measuring spoons.
- Balloons.
- Dish detergent.
- Empty cans and containers.
- Empty spools.
- Corks.
- Candles (I kept the matches in my desk).
- Toothpicks.
- A funnel.
- Rubber bands.
- An eyedropper.

Sharing Time

When the hard work—the investigating, researching, experimenting, discussing, organizing, writing, and illustrating—was done, then came the time we all loved. This was sharing time, when individuals or groups could share their findings, writings, drawings, or whatever else they had been working on. Sharing time was relaxed and friendly, not a time of stress. At first I thought I would pick one or two people each day to share. But I quickly discovered that everyone wanted to share every day. So we would sometimes have to share within groups or with peer partners. In this way, everyone who wanted to could have a chance to be heard.

The one rule I insisted on was that after each child shared, others in the class had to make at least one positive comment. Anyone who opened with a question or a criticism would quickly be asked to begin with a positive comment. Even the shyest students started to volunteer to share.

I also taped many of the sharing sessions. This made it a real occasion, and the presenters tried to use their best oral language skills. This was also a good way for me to evaluate students more effectively.

One unusually hot and humid day in late May, my class and I were doing our best to stay cool during science workshop. Small groups of students were huddled together, some reading from books about volcanos, others engaged in writing down information they had just read. Still other groups were talking about volcanos, sharing facts they had learned, and making group decisions about how to present this information to the class. Suddenly the intercom crackled and announced that there would be a show in the auditorium in ten minutes. Cheers could be heard from classrooms up and down the hall; there would be a reprieve from the heat and the schoolwork. But instead of the sigh of relief that I expected from my class, I heard: "Do we have to go?" "Can't we keep working on our science research?"

"You don't want to go?" I asked.

"We'd rather be doing science!" seemed to be the universal reply.

Thinking back to the questions I had had about science workshop, I knew that the children's response provided all the confirmation I needed. Students were making decisions, were totally involved, and were using the control they had been allowed to take to become active, involved, and committed to knowing more about science.

References

Alexander, A. and S. Bower. 1986. *Science magic: Scientific experiments for young children*. New York: Prentice-Hall for Young Readers.

Ardley, N. 1991. *The science book of air*. San Diego: Harcourt, Brace, Jovanovich.

Cobb, V. 1972. *Science experiments you can eat*. New York: J. B. Lippincott.

Cole, J. 1987. *The magic school bus inside the earth*. New York: Scholastic.

Gardner, M. 1981. *Entertaining science experiments with everyday objects*. New York: Dover.

Herbert, D. 1959. *Mr. Wizard's experiments for young children*. New York: Doubleday.

———. 1980. *Mr. Wizard's supermarket science*. New York: Random House.

Hoffman, J. 1989. *Backyard scientist*. Irvine, Calif.: Backyard Scientist.

McGill, O. 1984. *Science magic: 101 experiments you can do.* New York: Arco.

Ontario Science Center. 1984. *Science works.* Reading, Mass.: Addison-Wesley.

White, L. 1975. *Science tricks.* Reading, Mass.: Addison-Wesley.

———. 1984. *Science puzzles.* Reading, Mass.: Addison-Wesley.

4 Charles Pearce

What If . . . ?

Eagerly, the three of us removed the items from the box: a jug of water, a container of salt, several balls, a scale, clay, measuring devices, and a packet of activity cards. The instructions for our group of teachers in the Elementary Science Integration Project Summer Workshop were to spend the hour from 1:00 to 2:00 experiencing hands-on science, completing each activity, and writing about what we had done. Simply removing the contents was fun. As we examined and manipulated the materials we asked questions aloud and worked together with the contents to figure out, What if . . . ?

By 2:15 we realized that our time had expired. We also realized that we had not yet even started the assigned activities from the cards. The cards had been forgotten as we first tried our own activities and then designed ways to answer our own questions. Reporting back to the larger group at this summer science workshop, we apologetically indicated that somehow we had been sidetracked, seduced by the many possibilities posed by the materials, and had not completed the assigned activities. We had, however, made many discoveries and really enjoyed our time together.

What if, I thought while driving home that day, I tried giving fifth-grade students boxes of materials with no directions, no packets of activity cards? There would be no hidden agendas, no regimented steps to follow, no expected outcomes. Would learning take place? Could that learning be assessed? Would this approach encourage higher-level thinking and enable the students to monitor and evaluate thinking processes? Could the curriculum still be addressed if students were afforded a wide range of choices? What if . . . ?

Classroom science instruction might be viewed as a scale on which one far end is textbook instruction. As an elementary school student, I experienced science in class by reading chapters and answering textbook questions. Science was no fun.

Later we moved on to teacher demonstrations. This next step on the continuum was far more entertaining. We loved it when our science teacher performed experiments for us; it was almost like a magic show and we looked forward to her tricks.

After I became a teacher, the move across the scale toward hands-on science brought those experiments from the teacher's lab table to the students' desks. That, I thought at the time, was the best possible science instruction—lots of materials in the hands of the students as they followed well-planned directions from the teacher. Hands-on science was the mark of our progress since Sputnik, and this was the ultimate in classroom science.

But now, reflecting on the experiences of the summer workshop, I wanted to enable my students to take a more active role in the classroom. I wanted them to experience the same exhilaration that I had felt that afternoon when I had abandoned the activity cards, created my own questions, and then found the answers.

Approaching inquiry-based science instruction forced me to consider numerous procedural questions:

- How could I help my students develop their own testable questions?
- How could I foster active participation for all students?
- How could I keep up with the demands of inquiry-based science materials?
- How could I (and my students) be accountable for our time?
- How could I integrate science with writing and reading?
- How could I assess progress?
- How could my *I*'s become *we*'s so that all of us in the classroom would be collaborators with one another?

A more philosophical question also occurred to me, based on my own recognition that young children are scientists. Preschoolers, playing in the sandbox, are driven by their own need to find out. They want to explore their environment, discover how sand can cover objects or be molded into shapes. Their memories recall past play and enable further developments. Play for those children is true science at work. Yet at school, a child's expertise as a scientist is often discounted. Even hands-on science programs provide narrow structures, confining the budding scientist and discouraging divergence. My goal was to foster questioning and thinking; my own questions about science learning were sparking my thinking about science instruction.

Questions and Science

Science discovery is driven by questions. What we do is a response to the questions we are considering. Of greater importance is the consideration of who owns the questions. Where do they originate? Who really cares?

Recent research in language arts instruction has pointed toward an increased awareness of the role of the student as questioner. If students can ask appropriate questions after reading a story, comprehension is taking place.

It is natural for kids to ask questions. My goal was to help my students recognize that if they could ask the right questions, they could find the answers—often by collaborating with their peers. I began by modeling. Each day I thought aloud, asking questions of myself and my students:

- Will oil spilled in the ocean float? How do we know? Can we test that in our classroom?
- Are all rocks the same? How can any differences be measured?
- How is a #2 pencil different from a ballpoint pen?
- If acorns are seeds, will they sprout and grow?

To many of the questions I had no perfectly correct answers. With a high degree of tolerance, we listened to one another's attempts at explaining and answering. For the students to ask effective questions, they had to feel comfortable enough to take risks with new ideas. We soon discovered that a good question often serves as a catalyst for many others. We posted a sign in the room to affirm our confidence: "The best questions are our own questions."

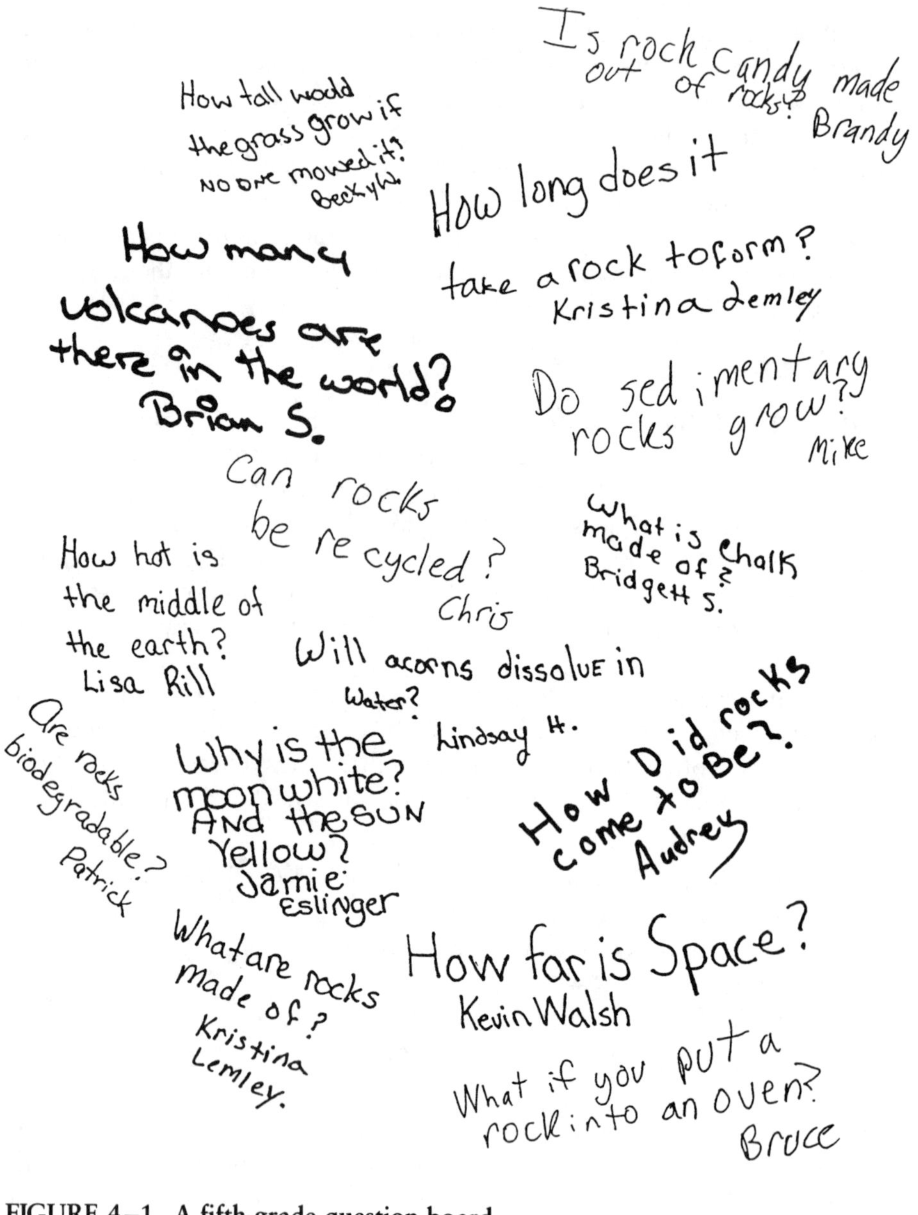

How tall would
the grass grow if
NO ONE mowed it?
Becky W.

Is rock candy made
out of rocks? Brandy

How long does it
take a rock to form?
Kristina Lemley

How many
volcanoes are
there in the world?
Brian S.

Do sedimentary
rocks grow?
Mike

Can rocks
be recycled?
Chris

What is chalk
made of?
Bridgett S.

How hot is
the middle of
the earth?
Lisa Rill

Will acorns dissolve in
Water?
Lindsay H.

How did rocks
come to Be?
Audrey

Are rocks
biodegradable?
Patrick

Why is the
moon white?
And the SUN
Yellow?
Jamie
Eslinger

What are rocks
made of?
Kristina
Lemley.

How far is Space?
Kevin Walsh

What if you put a
rock into an oven?
Bruce

FIGURE 4–1. A fifth-grade question board.

The Question Board

Questioning is the heart of inquiry science and, indeed, of science itself. Questions often arise for which a class has neither an immediate answer nor the time to investigate. In our class these questions were recorded on the "question board."

Early in the year we posted a large piece of laminated oak tag on which students could write whatever questions they wished. Although part of the magic might have been in using the overhead markers, the students seemed drawn to the question board for other reasons as well. This was a place where they could publicly share their own questions and read the questions of others. (Figure 4–1 shows one of our question boards.)

At first, the students wanted to know if they had to limit their questions to those related to science. Yet, upon examination of possible questions, they found that nearly *all* questions were science oriented in some way. Curriculum-based questions were interesting, of course, but we really wanted to encourage *any* questions the students were pondering.

Students wrote questions before and after class, or during class discussion when a question arose for which no one had an answer. By having the question board available early in the year, we examined the process of questioning and looked at types of questions.

Later, as the board was filled, a committee of students copied the questions for publication. The printed questions were used in our discussions of testable questions (i.e., those questions that students can answer by designing their own experiments). Although questions such as "How hot is the sun?" may not appear to be testable, one student pointed out that with the right tools, nearly *every* question about the physical world is testable.

This use of the question board enabled the students to examine their own questions and distinguish between those that could be readily tested and those that couldn't. Later, we used this experience to actually design our own experiments.

Thinking Scientifically

Putting students in control of their own learning enhances motivation. Kids who make choices or design activities are kids who think about learning. This process internalizes values and provides ownership for the learner.

My work in teaching thinking was premised on two assumptions. First, I realized that activities that were not teacher directed would require

far more thought than directed activities. Activities for which students had
to tap their prior knowledge and create their own questions entailed more
thought than those that required only answers or the completion of blanks
on a ditto sheet. Second, I assumed that *all* students could think at these
levels, especially if taught how to do so. However, direct instruction in
problem solving might not be beneficial. To engage students in authentic
scientific thinking, the problems under consideration had to emanate from
the students themselves. In a sense, I had to avoid directly teaching thinking
skills in isolation in order to teach thinking skills in context.

Activities used in language arts, when applied to science instruction,
proved helpful in this regard. In activities like know-wonder-learn (see
Figure 4–2) students first list five things they know about a topic, then five
questions they have, and later (after reading or doing an activity) five things
they have learned. This activity links prior knowledge with new knowledge.
I understood that without tapping prior knowledge, inquiry science would

KNOW – WONDER – LEARN   TOPIC Mealworms   NAME Jamie + Jenny

DIRECTIONS- 1) Write five things you know about the topic in the KNOW column.
2) Write five things you wonder about in the WONDER column.
3) READ the story or LISTEN to the presentation.
4) After the story or presentation write five things you learned in the LEARN column.

KNOW	WONDER	LEARN
1. THey eat oatmeal.	1. How Big can they get?	1. They are eating all the time.
2. They have small eggs.	2. How old are they when they Become a bug?	2. The eggs are so small you hardly see them.
3. THey are a worm.	3. How many colors can they be?	3. They are tan, brown, and sort of white.
4. They slither.	4. How many colors can they be?	4. They're fun to work with.
5.	5.	5.

FIGURE 4–2. A know-wonder-learn activity on mealworms.

be like a bottle set adrift, hollow and disconnected. (Blank forms for many of the activities discussed here are included in the Appendix to this chapter. They are suitable for you to reproduce, and you may feel free to do so.)

Reciprocal teaching (Palinsar and Brown 1986, Coley and DePinto 1989) was another idea that could be utilized. Students in small groups had been discussing and summarizing what was already known, questioning one another, identifying and clarifying what might be confusing if younger students were present, and predicting outcomes or what might happen next. These think tanks were great for language classes and proved effective in science as well.

As the students gained confidence in questioning and problem solving, they were no longer merely recipients of facts and directions, and I was no longer the only decision maker in the room. Our roles began to change. I wasn't sure how comfortable I was with what was happening. Although I still hoped to devise a formal means of assessing my own success and the students' progress, in the meantime certain informal hints kept me going.

A new student had just joined our class. As I welcomed him, I invited the other students to assist in explaining our system and how we viewed science. Charlotte told the new student that he was lucky to be in our class because now, just like the rest of us, he was a scientist. As I looked about and saw the others nodding their approval, I realized that what we had gained could not be measured by conventional means. Something good was definitely happening.

Inquiry science, however, is more than asking questions and thinking like a scientist; rather it is a spiral of questioning, thinking, testing, recording, and questioning again. The teacher's role is to provide a workable framework for all of this activity. In our classroom, that framework was provided by the "discovery boxes."

If You Make Them, They Will Use Them

Discovery boxes were the major component of inquiry science in our classroom and were developed as a direct result of my experiences at the Elementary Science Integration Project Summer Workshop. These cardboard boxes contained related items on a particular theme. (See the Appendix for examples of what might be included in some of these boxes.) In conjunction with the use of the question board, the discovery boxes were a natural extension for real-life, hands-on inquiry. Once children felt comfortable developing testable questions, the boxes served as a resource to help them as they investigated their questions.

Each discovery box contained a number of items to aid students as they designed experiments. Trade books on the theme of the box provided background and often sparked new questions. Materials useful in testing, safe for independent use, and related to the theme were collected; our goal was to offer possibilities rather than restrictions. An essential part of each box was a folder in which students recorded information. (See the example of a completed discovery log in Figure 4–3.) This folder reinforced the concept that with the freedom of exploration and investigation comes the responsibility of documentation. The records in the folder served not only as a means of accountability, but also as a way for students to communicate with one another as scientific colleagues.

Finding topics for the discovery boxes was not difficult but deciding which topics to develop was a challenge. Many of the topics arose from questions on the question board; others were related to the fifth-grade curriculum. But we did not limit our inquiry to the prescribed fifth-grade

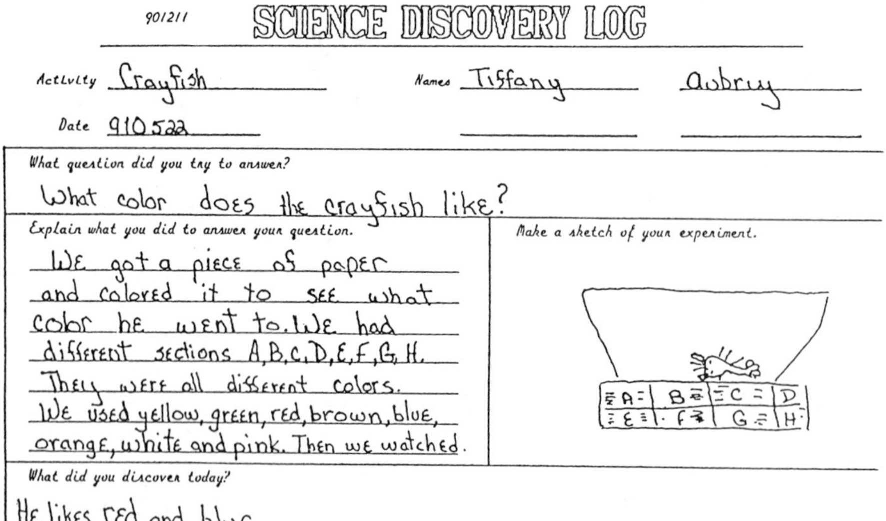
901211 SCIENCE DISCOVERY LOG

Activity: Crayfish
Names: Tiffany, Aubrey
Date: 910522

What question did you try to answer?
What color does the crayfish like?

Explain what you did to answer your question.
We got a piece of paper and colored it to see what color he went to. We had different sections A, B, C, D, E, F, G, H. They were all different colors. We used yellow, green, red, brown, blue, orange, white and pink. Then we watched.

Make a sketch of your experiment.

What did you discover today?
He likes red and blue.

What new question are you curious about for another time? Does he like bright or dark places?

Are you pleased with your results today? YES ✓ NO ___ NOT SURE ___

How would your group rate this activity? Great (10) 9 8 7 6 5 4 3 2 1 0 Terrible

FIGURE 4–3. A completed discovery log for a crayfish activity.

subjects. One day Brian asked, "What would happen if I hooked up five batteries to one flashlight bulb?" He was putting to use his knowledge from last year's science class in which they had studied electricity. It is not only natural for kids to want to carry on with ideas from previous years, but also encouraging. There is no reason why kids hooked on magnets in third grade should not continue to explore magnetism in the fourth or fifth grade. Children's interests do not turn on and off with the end of a unit or a grade. Topics investigated in our class this year included magnets, electricity, liquids, mealworms, soils, and rocks and minerals.

For instance, included in the "liquid" box were a variety of measuring instruments and containers, liquids such as water, oil, and vinegar, food coloring, pH paper, sugar, salt, filter paper, soil, and more. Also included were possible questions for students to attempt to answer (although they should be encouraged to investigate their own questions). With tubs and buckets (and a sink, if one is available) the children will immediately be able to begin manipulating the materials.

The mealworm box contained straws, pipe cleaners, string, colored construction paper, and, of course, mealworms. These creatures can be obtained inexpensively from most pet shops and are the perfect animal for classroom investigation. Students enjoy the mealworms by observing how they react to edges and obstructions, or by seeing which colors they prefer.

Included with the discovery boxes were back-up boxes. In the spiral of questioning and investigating, kids develop many ideas. It is difficult to predict what questions will be pursued and what additional materials may be needed by young investigators. My goal was to have on hand what the students would need when a hot topic was being investigated. Thus I provided several resource boxes to supplement the materials in the discovery boxes. The resource boxes contained materials that were useful and versatile. Among those materials were aluminum foil, pipe cleaners, flexible straws, rigid straws, clay, and toothpicks. There were neither directions nor suggestions, simply possibilities. The students always found interesting ways to use whatever was provided.

How and When

Time is the most challenging aspect of inquiry-based science. When in the day can the kids go off and explore their own interests? And in a class of twenty-five or thirty students, how can this be organized? After a bit of experimentation, the students and I developed the "inquiry period."

CHOICES FOR:
TUESDAY, DEC. 10

A. LIQUIDS BOX   Dawn C   Paige   Kristina

B. ELECTRICITY BOX   Kevin W.   Brooks S   _____

C. MEALWORMS BOX   Julie C.   Tiffany D   _____

D. SOILS BOX   Corey S.   _____   _____

E. ROCKS & MINERALS BOX   Jennifer L   Lindsay H.   _____

F. MAGNETISM BOX   Ginger T.   Sarah R.   _____

G. HOURGLASS WORKSHOP   Jamie L   Jenny Bundra   _____

H. TOWER WORKSHOP   Anton   Jacob   _____

I. FILMSTRIP WORKSHOP   Bridgett S.   Jeff Miller   Charis T.

J. MEDIA CENTER   Jamie S.   Lisa R.   _____

K. _____   _____   _____   _____

L. _____   _____   _____   _____

M. _____   _____   _____   _____

N. _____   _____   _____   _____

O. _____   _____   _____   _____

P. _____   _____   _____   _____

Q. _____   _____   _____   _____

R. _____   _____   _____   _____

FIGURE 4–4. A sign-up list for an inquiry period.

An inquiry period, which might occur several times a week, was a forty-minute time block in which groups of two or three students worked together on activities of their own choosing. A day or two in advance, students signed up for specific activities chosen from a list (see Figure 4–4). Then, during the inquiry period, they worked together on those activities.

A few ground rules proved helpful. First, students were expected to stay with their selected activities. It is best to avoid having children jump from one thing to another, thus losing their focus. Quietly reading or observing what others are doing is acceptable for those who finish early or lose interest. However, the students should know they are accountable for their time. In addition to log sheets (see Figures 4–5 and 4–6), journal entries, or other written documentation, I often distributed What I Accomplished forms (see Figure 4–7) at the end of the period. These forms enabled students to summarize what they had done and helped me assess how they used their time.

The inquiry period gave me the opportunity to visit with small groups of students as they embarked on their own investigations. By asking questions or engaging in dialogue, I was able to participate in the activities with the children. The time I spent with each small group enabled me to give more personal attention and provided valuable feedback for assessment.

Later, we would have a class discussion during which a representative of each group reported to the class. This time for sharing helped to focus each group's accomplishments and to heighten interest within the class for each group's investigations. Since the sharing time was limited, students were encouraged to learn more by reading the Body of Knowledge and the Science Discovery Log forms (see Appendix).

The Science and Writing Connection

One exciting result of the popularity of the discovery boxes was the enhancement of communication skills used to record and share student discoveries. Scientific writing by the students took many forms. Recording data on the log sheets in the discovery boxes was just a beginning; students also wrote in journals, in the class Body of Knowledge booklet, and in writing workshop. They wrote for different audiences and for different purposes.

Just as journals had been used in language arts to share and comment upon student ideas concerning books, activities, and events to remember, journals were used for scientific thinking on paper. Journal entries included discussions of ideas and experiments performed with materials in

INQUIRY PERIOD LOG SHEET   920103

Name Charis Fulton   Date Jan. 10, 1992

Activity HourGlass

Who did you work with today? Paige

Describe your activity.

We made hour glasses by putting
salt in soda bottles. Two soda caps
were put together to hold the two
soda bottles.

How did you use your time?

When we made hour glasses we
timed them to see how long they
took. The firt one we did took
4 min. and 25 seconds. The hole inside
the soda caps was $\frac{3}{4}$.

What did you find particularly interesting about today's activity?

Measuring how much salt was in the hour glass was neat.
The 2nd one we did the hole was bigger
so the sand came out a lot faster and
we put a lot more salt in it to. There
was two cups of sand in it.

Convince someone else that your activity was a worthwhile use of school time.

This morning in school when we had Inquiry
Period I had a lot of fun. This activity wasn't
a waste of time. I know now more about it.
I know that theres about 2 cups of salt
in the soda bottles if you are using a cap with a
$\frac{5}{16}$ hole in it and the hour glass will take 1 min.
and 7 seconds. Hour glasses are fun to work
with and they're very helpfull with telling
telling the time.

FIGURE 4–5. A completed inquiry period log sheet.

LOG SHEET

NAMES *Jacob   Brooks Jeff*

DATE *Jan. 10, 1992*

SKETCHES

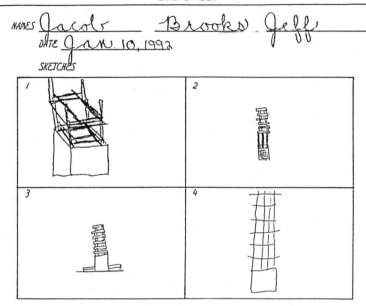

Which design or combination seemed the most stable?

number 1

How high was your tallest tower today? __5__ *feet* __4__ *inches*

Describe the construction of your tallest or favorite tower design.
(If it is not shown above, sketch on back.)

I used blocks to support blocks standing up right holding up other blocks

FIGURE 4–6. A completed tower workshop log sheet.

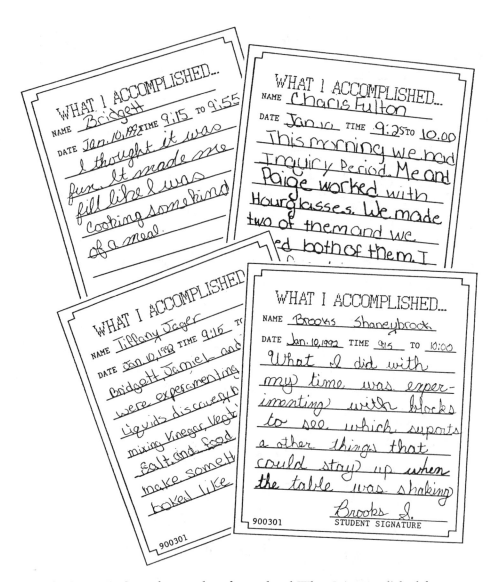

FIGURE 4–7. Several examples of completed What I Accomplished forms.

discovery boxes, as well as thoughts or questions for further exploration. Moreover, journal entries allowed the students to talk to me on paper and afforded me a place to record my responses. For scientists, an important feature of journal writing is its permanence. Both the students and I could return to read previous entries again and again.

900801

BODY OF KNOWLEDGE
STUDENT DISCOVERED FACTS

Page __1__

NO.	DATE	FACT	HOW THIS WAS DISCOVERED	SCIENTIST(S)
1	9-12-91	Oil floats on rain water.	We mixed them together.	Brad
2	Sep 12	If you hook a tiny light Bulb to two 6 volts Batteries it will Burn out	It was tested by Batteries, wires, and a light Bulb	Matt
3	9/13/91	If you put a mealworm on a pipe cleaner, he will hang upside down.	We tested it by puttin them on a pipe cleaner upside down	Tom
4	9-14	If you shake distilled water and saltwater the saltwater will bubble more	I turned a jug of saltwater and distilled water upside down and the saltwater got more bubbly.	Brandy S

FIGURE 4–8. The first page of a class Body of Knowledge booklet.

One innovation our class used for recording data was the Body of Knowledge booklet in which students entered their own discoveries (see Figure 4–8). This booklet provided a place for recording and sharing information; it is a key to developing a community of student scientists. As a public record, it enabled each student to publish discoveries for others and to get feedback, encouragement, and new ideas.

The science and writing connection was also forged through our writing workshop. Our discovery boxes provided real-life topics and stories for students to write about. The relative quiet and reflective nature of that time enabled students to think in depth about their science experience. Science process and content were intriguing fodder for the workshop. Some students even wrote books. One picture book that approached science with humor was *The Pyrite Who Thought He Was Gold*. This story (reproduced in Figure 4–9) related the tale of a resident of Rockville, his delusions of grandeur, embarrassment, and eventual acceptance of his true identity.

FIGURE 4–9. *The Pyrite Who Thought He Was Gold.*

Rocks started to ask him to prove it. Pyrite didn't know what to do.

The rocks stopped calling him gold. Pyrite thought about proving himself as gold.

He went to a rock specialist to find the truth.

The specialist did lots of tests.

FIGURE 4-9 (continued).

He did the color test, streak test, vinegar test, magnet test, electrical test and, the luster test. The hardness test proved that he was pyrite, not gold.

It proved that he was pyrite. He was very embarrassed. He went back to Rockville, unhappily.

He didn't talk for a few weeks because of his awful discovery. Then one day his best friend limestone came up to talk to him.

He told Pyrite that he didn't care if he was Pyrite or gold. That made Pyrite feel better.

So then Prite didn't care about how he looked any more. He was happy the way he was!

FIGURE 4–9 (continued).

This book passed through many steps before Hannah, Julie, and Tiffany were ready to publish it—with a sparkling cover of their own design as well as illustrations. Writing and science were linked for them in an authentic way, and their product was a result of their own choices.

The Science and Reading Connection

Even more intriguing was the way the inquiry approach with the discovery boxes encouraged independent reading of a variety of trade books. Although the books in the boxes were seldom used during the excitement of an inquiry period, the books were read with interest when a part of each day was set aside for quiet, independent reading. We used DEAR (Drop Everything And Read) time for students to read materials of their own choosing. Students often selected books from boxes they planned to investigate in the next inquiry period or from boxes they had just used. In addition to reading trade books from the boxes and from our class library, students used DEAR time to read from the Body of Knowledge. They enjoyed seeing what others had discovered and found that reading others' work enhanced the development of their own questions.

New Aisles in the Library

Student inquiry in the classroom also influenced book selection at the library. By investigating their own questions, students were motivated to seek books that might help answer specific questions or that might give clues toward solving a particular problem. I felt quite comfortable when reading time was spent finding and reading science books. From their real-life experiences, students were motivated to think about topics, find books at the library based on their interests, and then use what they had read to shape further inquiry. This process of learning is similar to the way adults learn—not by fulfilling someone else's assigned work, but by engaging in experiences that truly interest and can yield further questions and journeys of inquiry.

Links to Literature

Sarah had been reading *Hello, Mrs. Piggle-Wiggle*, by Betty MacDonald (1957). In the story, Melody is considered a crybaby by her friends and family; the smallest incident starts her crying. One evening at dinner Melody's tears really flow.

"I've never seen so many tears in my life," her father said. "How in the world did you do it?"

"I don't know," Melody said. "I just started to cry and the tears came out."

"I'm going to rent you out to water lawns," her daddy said.

"Salt water kills grass," Cornell said.

This was where Sarah stopped. She wanted to know if salt water really did kill grass.

Sarah remembered our minilesson on testable questions. She decided that her question was indeed testable. But it also yielded many other questions.

"We can try watering grass with salt water," Sarah said, "but how much salt should we use? How salty are tears? How salty is the ocean?"

Even though it wasn't science time, Sarah was able to immediately record her questions on the question board. Later, she went on to design a study of grass and salt water.

Providing opportunities for links throughout the day is one outcome of this integrated approach.

Science, Technology, and Kids

The link between science and technology is portrayed in an entertaining way by James Burke in his PBS series *Connections*. Weaving his way through history, Burke shows how each seemingly minor scientific discovery is linked to the next in a progression that has led to many of our present technological marvels. Science is portrayed as being useful.

Recreating these kinds of authentic experiences in the classroom has been one goal of our inquiry system. If we can make our own discoveries technologically useful, we can provide purpose for our inquiry.

One day Adam came to school very excited about some rocks he had found in the woods behind his house.

"I think they are calcite," he said as we carefully examined each one.

"How do you know?" I asked.

"Well, they look like those calcite rocks from when we worked with rocks and minerals."

"Yes they do," I agreed, "but how can we tell for sure?"

"We could use vinegar to see if they fizz," Adam suggested.

I was a bit surprised. Adam was a student who was a challenge to motivate, yet he had apparently remembered what we had done several months earlier as we explored mineral testing and identification.

Adam put a few pieces of his rocks into a small plastic cup and poured some vinegar over them so that they were submerged. Sure enough, they began to bubble. Everyone was impressed with Adam's success.

"Maybe," Adam said, "I could make a discovery box with my calcite and vinegar and other things for kids to work with. They could try doing other things, too." I liked Adam's idea and suggested he begin work during our next inquiry period. But the story was just beginning.

Like one of those mistakes or accidents that led to scientific discoveries in the past, Adam's plastic cup was set aside and forgotten. The following Monday morning Adam discovered that the vinegar had evaporated and a white material was covering the calcite.

"That must be chalk," he announced.

"Why do you say that?" someone else asked.

"Well, isn't chalk calcium carbonate?" he asked.

"Is it?" I asked, surprised again with Adam's knowledge.

"Yes, it is," some others answered.

"Calcite is, too," Adam said. "This white stuff must be chalk!"

With that, he took a piece of the white material and wrote his name on the board. Though it crumbled in his hand, Adam had indeed used the material as chalk.

Then Adam made that technological link. He planned to go back to his woods, mine more calcite, crush it, mix it with vinegar, wait for the vinegar to evaporate, and make chalk to sell. He would implement his plan from raw materials to processed product and then market his product for profit. Based on a data base of prior knowledge, Adam was taking a technological journey.

Adam formed a small group to assist in his "chalk company." He lost interest in the discovery box idea (which was OK), and his chalk company had some serious manufacturing problems, but the process was unfolding in a way that Adam would never forget.

Scientific inquiry for Adam and his group continued as they struggled with possible binding agents to keep their chalk from crumbling. Their experiments yielded other products. One "failure" for chalk produced a by-product much like concrete.

Though the year ended with no profits earned, the chalk company had touched upon many objectives of our science and social studies curriculums.

We later found an 800 number for Binney and Smith, makers of Crayola™ chalk. Adam planned to call them over the summer to see how they made noncrumbling chalk. Whatever the result, Adam's interest and motivation were apparent.

Assessment

As my view of science instruction evolved, my concept of assessment likewise began to change.

How could I use those prepared tests of factual knowledge when our inquiry-based instruction stressed higher-level thinking and greater student involvement in the actual planning of many activities? How could I reliably assess student progress in this changing environment?

Our school system's science curriculum contained behavioral objectives that stressed the importance of observing hands-on activities as a means of assessment. It seemed logical that assessing progress in scientific thinking could likewise be accomplished by viewing the outcomes, the products of this inquiry-based approach. Looking for divergent results precluded the use of formulaic evaluation. I had to creatively evaluate my own assessment methods.

Since inquiry focuses on questions, I first looked carefully at the questions being developed by my students. I read the questions on the question board. Who was asking the questions? What kinds of questions were they? I then looked for student questions in log books and science notebooks. I read through the Body of Knowledge and the Science Discovery Log sheets in the discovery box folders. I looked at the inquiry period sign-up sheets. I also began what has been termed "kid watching" (Goodman 1978). I observed and recorded who was doing what. This approach may not have provided the quantitative data of traditional testing, but it gave me a subjective feel for the quality of thinking taking place among my students.

I also modified those traditional tests to provide authentic evaluation. Factual recall was not totally discarded, but all tests became open-folder ones since I did not want merely to evaluate memory skills. I added questions that asked students to design experiments for specific problems or questions. Some tests simply asked students to write questions rather than answer them. A content analysis of question levels helped me to determine how sophisticated those questions were.

I also began using work from writing workshop to assess progress (and derive grades) for science.

A further assessment concept with intriguing possibilities is using students to assess and evaluate themselves. As they observe the investigations of others and read about their discoveries, they naturally evaluate the credibility of their fellow students. Evaluating one another's progress would provide valuable feedback to adjust and fine-tune further inquiry.

This assessment approach could never be computerized or empirically calculated, but I began to feel that I could reliably assess student progress. By knowing my students and using their reactions to what we were doing in the classroom, I felt I could evaluate them effectively.

What Next?

There is an underlying attitude that stretches beyond the components of this inquiry-based approach to science. The components of our program are not really new or especially innovative. Yet, when combined with an attitude that science is questioning and the best questions come from students, this approach can make any youngster into a scientist. And this attitude is contagious. When Charlotte welcomed the new student as a fellow scientist, she was communicating that attitude. When the others plugged into the system their own interests and ideas and questions, when they participated by choosing, they were buying into that system and embracing that attitude. They felt good about themselves and their role as student scientists.

These components of the inquiry-based system are still undergoing change and adjustment. The system itself is anything but a well-oiled machine. There was a time when this would have caused me great concern, but as this science instruction has been evolving I have come to realize that the link between inquiry and instruction requires flexibility. From student-chosen discovery boxes, to student-created discovery boxes, from trade books students read to trade books students create, inquiry science is about growth and change—for teachers as well as students.

The notion of the discovery box as the epitome of science instruction was dispelled when Adam asked if he could make his own discovery box for others to use. I had not considered the possibility of students providing boxes of materials along particular themes. Along that continuum from teacher-assigned textbook pages and questions to student-developed discovery boxes I can't help wondering what the next step will be.

Building upon the discoveries of others has been the key to progress in our scientifically oriented, technological society. Fashioning science in our classrooms to resemble the real-life connections of scientific progress is our challenge for the future. Just as scientists of long ago are still able to communicate to us through their writings, students from previous years can communicate to future students in their own words through journals, our Body of Knowledge, and other writing. This reading/writing process is authentic, self-motivating, and exciting.

One plan we have for this enhanced communication is a five-year project in which students design an ideal, sealed terrarium in which life forms can survive for an extended period with nothing except sunlight. What combination of plants and animals will be just right? Students will be able to experiment and record results so that future students can progress farther toward a specific goal. When students graduate at the end of the year, they will leave behind their discoveries for others to build upon. This is science in its truest form. Students questioning and discovering, publishing results, utilizing what has been learned to push the frontier even further—students actually becoming scientists.

Incorporating inquiry science in a workshop setting does not necessarily mean discarding more traditional approaches. In today's science classroom there is still a place for textbooks (as resources), student/teacher lecture for key concepts that may not lend themselves to the inquiry approach (or to provide prior knowledge), or student/teacher demonstrations for efficient use of time and materials. Certainly, teacher-directed, hands-on instruction is important as a jumping-off point for inquiry that may follow, but we should not limit ourselves to this level.

Providing the least restrictive environment for all students means providing opportunities for children to design their own learning in a carefully administered environment. This approach is being used in many classrooms and can be added to others. A commitment to enhanced thinking not only carries over skills to all subject areas but will increase performance on the new generation of standardized tests that have progressed beyond simple recall.

In addition, we will be providing society with kids who can think scientifically even if many will not go on to become professional scientists. It is important for youngsters in our educational system to be able to follow directions, but that is not enough. Kids who can write their own directions are the ones who will be equipped to tackle the problems of our technological society, the problems of the twenty-first century and beyond.

References

Coley, J. D., and T. DePinto. 1989. Merging reciprocal teaching with question response cues. *Reading: Issues & Practices* 6: 76–80.

Goodman, Y. 1978. Kid watching: An alternative to testing. *National Elementary School Principal* 57: 41–45.

MacDonald, B. 1957. *Hello, Mrs. Piggle-Wiggle.* New York: Scholastic.

Palinsar, A. M., and A. L. Brown. 1986. Interactive teaching to promote independent learning from text. *Reading Teacher* 39(8): 771–77.

Appendix 4–1
Reproducible Forms

KNOW - WONDER - LEARN

TOPIC _____   NAME _____

DIRECTIONS- 1) Write five things you know about the topic in the KNOW column.
2) Write five things you wonder about in the WONDER column.
3) READ the story or LISTEN to the presentation.
4) After the story or presentation write five things you learned in the LEARN column.

KNOW	WONDER	LEARN
1.	1.	1.
2.	2.	2.
3.	3.	3.
4.	4.	4.
5.	5.	5.

SCIENCE DISCOVERY LOG

901211

Activity _____

Names _____

Date _____

What question did you try to answer?

Explain what you did to answer your question.

Make a sketch of your experiment.

What did you discover today?

What new question are you curious about for another time?

Are you pleased with your results today?   YES ___   NO ___   NOT SURE ___

How would your group rate this activity?   Great 10   9   8   7   6   5   4   3   2   1   0   Terrible

CHOICES FOR:

A.

B.

C.

D.

E.

F.

G.

H.

I.

J.

K.

L.

M.

N.

O.

P.

Q.

R.

INQUIRY PERIOD LOG SHEET

920/03

Name _____   Date _____

Activity _____

Who did you work with today? _____   _____

_____   _____

Describe your activity.

How did you use your time?

What did you find particularly interesting about today's activity?

Convince someone else that your activity was a worthwhile use of school time.

920102 # TOWER WORKSHOP

LOG SHEET

NAMES _____ _____ _____

DATE _____

SKETCHES

1	2
3	4

Which design or combination seemed the most stable?

How high was your tallest tower today?   ____feet ____inches

Describe the construction of your tallest or favorite tower design.
(If it is not shown above, sketch on back.)

WHAT I ACCOMPLISHED...

NAME _____

DATE _____ TIME _____ TO _____

_____
_____
_____
_____
_____
_____
_____

_____
STUDENT SIGNATURE

900301

WHAT I ACCOMPLISHED...

NAME _____

DATE _____ TIME _____ TO _____

_____
_____
_____
_____
_____
_____
_____

_____
STUDENT SIGNATURE

900301

BODY OF KNOWLEDGE
STUDENT DISCOVERED FACTS

900801

Page _____

NO.	DATE	QUESTION	FACT	SCIENTIST(S)

SCIENCE DISCOVERY

ELECTRICITY DISCOVERY BOX

Some materials you may find in this discovery box:
- batteries (various sizes and ages)
- bulbs and holders
- wire
- various conductors and insulators
- electrical components

(Other materials for investigation can be found in boxes #1 and 2.)

DIRECTIONS
1. Consider a question that you would like to answer. You may select a question from those below or you may develop your own question.
2. Read some of the Science Discovery Log forms in this folder to see what other student scientists have discovered.
3. Begin a Science Discovery Log form of your own.
4. Conduct your investigation.
5. Complete the Science Discovery Log form that you started.
6. Add what you have discovered to the Body of Knowledge.

Some questions you may want to investigate:
- Which batteries make the bulbs light brighter?
- Which batteries last longer?
- How can you wire circuits in different ways?
- Can you make a switch?
- How can we make the light get dim and bright?
- How many bulbs will one battery light?
- Will electricity go through water? salt water? colored water?
- Can you light the bulb without using a battery?

Remember, the best questions are your own questions!
Be curious! Be creative! Have fun! ! !

SCIENCE DISCOVERY

MEALWORMS DISCOVERY BOX

Some materials you may find in this discovery box:
- mealworms
- oatmeal
- construction paper (various colors)
- string
- toothpicks
- straws

(Other materials for investigation can be found in boxes #1 and 2.)

DIRECTIONS

1. Consider a question that you would like to answer. You may select a question from those below or you may develop your own question.
2. Read some of the Science Discovery Log forms in this folder to see what other student scientists have discovered.
3. Begin a Science Discovery Log form of your own.
4. Conduct your investigation.
5. Complete the Science Discovery Log form that you started.
6. Add what you have discovered to the Body of Knowledge.

Some questions you may want to investigate:
- What colors do mealworms prefer?
- What do mealworms do when they come to an edge?
- How do mealworms behave when they are trapped?
- Which size mealworms are the fastest?
- Can mealworms be trained?
- What foods do mealworms like?
- Will mealworms walk uphill? How high can they climb?
- How do mealworms respond to certain chemicals?
- Are mealworms social?

Remember, the best questions are your own questions!
Be curious! Be creative! Have fun! ! !

SCIENCE DISCOVERY

MAGNETISM DISCOVERY BOX

Some materials you may find in this discovery box:

- magnets
- magnetic items
- iron filings
- wire
- flat materials of varying thicknesses
- sand
- salt

(Other materials for investigation can be found in boxes #1 and 2.)

DIRECTIONS

1. Consider a question that you would like to answer. You may select a question from those below or you may develop your own question.
2. Read some of the Science Discovery Log forms in this folder to see what other student scientists have discovered.
3. Begin a Science Discovery Log form of your own.
4. Conduct your investigation.
5. Complete the Science Discovery Log form that you started.
6. Add what you have discovered to the Body of Knowledge.

Some questions you may want to investigate:

- How are magnetic items similar?
- Do magnets have different strengths? If so, how can those strengths be compared and measured?
- How can magnets be used to accomplish work?
- How do magnets work?
- Can magnetic forces be transmitted through wires?
- Can magnetic forces go through paper? through cardboard? through water? through other materials?
- Can magnets be used to make electricity?
- How can magnets be made stronger?

Remember, the best questions are your own questions!
Be curious! Be creative! Have fun! ! !

SCIENCE DISCOVERY

LIQUIDS DISCOVERY BOX

Some materials you may find in this discovery box:

- various containers (some graduated, some marked A, B, C, etc.)
- paper cups
- vegetable oil
- salt
- sugar cubes
- food coloring
- gravel
- eye droppers
- construction paper
- vinegar
- pH paper
- thermometer
- clay
- coffee filters
- strainer
- straws
- soil samples

(Other materials for investigation can be found in boxes #1 and 2.)

DIRECTIONS

1. Consider a question that you would like to answer. You may select a question from those below or you may develop your own question.
2. Read some of the Science Discovery Log forms in this folder to see what other student scientists have discovered.
3. Begin a Science Discovery Log form of your own.
4. Conduct your investigation.
5. Complete the Science Discovery Log form that you started.
6. Add what you have discovered to the Body of Knowledge.

Some questions you may want to investigate:

- What evidence can you find to prove that dirty water can be cleaned?
- How can we purify salt water?
- What does pH paper tell us about certain liquids?
- Why do you think some materials dissolve while others do not?
- What if food coloring is placed in water but not stirred?
- What can we infer about water temperature and how materials dissolve?
- Will the same materials dissolve in water, vinegar, and oil?
- How are water, vinegar, and oil similar? How are they different?
- Which is the better lubricant, oil or water?

Remember, the best questions are your own questions!
Be curious! Be creative! Have fun! ! !

SCIENCE DISCOVERY

SOILS DISCOVERY BOX

Some materials you may find in this discovery box:
- powdered clay
- humus
- sand
- sifter
- hand lens
- gravel
- small jugs (for shaking)
- seeds
- containers

DIRECTIONS

1. Consider a question that you would like to answer. You may select a question from those below or you may develop your own question.
2. Read some of the Science Discovery Log forms in this folder to see what other student scientists have discovered.
3. Begin a Science Discovery Log form of your own.
4. Conduct your investigation.
5. Complete the Science Discovery Log form that you started.
6. Add what you have discovered to the Body of Knowledge.

Some questions you may want to investigate:
- Which soil type holds water the best?
- What if each soil type were mixed in water? Would any dissolve?
- What evidence can you find that soils come from rocks, plant and animal remains, or other things from the earth?
- How are any of these soils similar to soil around your house?
- Which soil type can be shaped into a ball when wet? when dry?
- Will rocks wear away faster in plain water, salt water, or sandy water?
- Design an improved way to control soil erosion.
- Which soil type (or combination) is best for growing plants?
- Design a new use for soil.

Remember, the best questions are your own questions!
Be curious! Be creative! Have fun! ! !

SCIENCE DISCOVERY

ROCKS & MINERALS DISCOVERY BOX

Some materials you may find in this discovery box:

- rock samples
- pennies, nails, glass jar (for hardness test)
- ceramic plate (for streak test)
- magnet
- battery, wires, bulb (for electrical test)
- vinegar and eye dropper
- sandpaper
- hand lens

DIRECTIONS

1. Consider a question that you would like to answer. You may select a question from those below or you may develop your own question.
2. Read some of the Science Discovery Log forms in this folder to see what other student scientists have discovered.
3. Begin a Science Discovery Log form of your own.
4. Conduct your investigation.
5. Complete the Science Discovery Log form that you started.
6. Add what you have discovered to the Body of Knowledge.

Some questions you may want to investigate:
- Combine the rock samples into groups that:
  - • are the same hardness,
  - • react to vinegar,
  - • look the same.
- Why do you think rocks are different?
- What does vinegar tell us about rocks?
- Assess the value of the rock samples by grouping from most valuable to least valuable.
- How can we improve methods of rock testing?

Remember, the best questions are your own questions!
Be curious! Be creative! Have fun! ! !

SCIENCE DISCOVERY

WHEN USING THE DISCOVERY BOX, PLEASE LOG YOUR NAME AND DATE AND INDICATE IF YOU COMPLETED A DISCOVERY LOG FORM.

Name	Date	Log form completed (✔)

5 Dana Blackwood

Connecting Language and Science Assessment

ESIP: Elementary Science Integration Project. Of those four words, only one troubled me, and that was the "S" word. It was pure and simple; science scared me. I thought of science as a body of knowledge with lists of factual information to be memorized and then used in some mysterious ways that were far beyond my level of understanding. So I became a member of ESIP with the hope that no one would discover the truth about science and me: I didn't know the facts!

Part of our work in ESIP involved identifying a topic for teacher research. I chose "assessment and evaluation" and began where I tell the learners in my class to begin, that is, with what they know. Could the alternative forms of assessment and evaluation that I used in language arts become the basis for evaluation and assessment in science? I quickly realized that my comfort with whole language assessment sprang in large part from my familiarity with the processes of reading, writing, speaking, and listening and with the developmental learning of language. My discomfort with science assessment and evaluation, I reasoned, came from a lack of understanding of science processes.

Although unfamiliar with science processes per se, I had heard about "the scientific method," a phrase that seemed to refer to the steps that scientists go through in solving problems. That sounded like science process, and I figured that all I had to do was to find out what those science processes were and use them as the basis of science assessment and evaluation. It did not seem complicated at all.

In truth, my search for the scientific method was not complicated; it was impossible! I began by asking several science educators and a scientist what the steps were, but no one could tell me. People were vague, said that they couldn't remember how many steps there were or couldn't remember the precise order of the steps. I felt discouraged; perhaps there was a scientific method club, an elite organization of people who knew the scientific method and had taken a vow of secrecy, swearing never to tell a nonmember of the club what the steps were; I was clearly to be excluded from the club forever.

My active imagination eventually gave way to reason as I returned to what I knew about whole language. I had worked hard and continue to work to understand reading and writing and oral language processes, so why did I expect a shortcut to understanding science processes?

I decided to educate myself. My plan was to collect any science process information that I could find and compare and analyze my data. I began by reading a booklet published by the Phi Delta Kappa Educational Foundation (Rakow 1986), which included a list of "science process skills" attributed to Science—A Process Approach (SAPA):

Basic Process Skills (introduced in grades K–3)
1. Observing
2. Classifying
3. Using space/time relationships
4. Using numbers
5. Communicating
6. Measuring
7. Predicting
8. Inferring

Integrated Process Skills (introduced in grades 4–6)
9. Formulating hypotheses
10. Controlling variables
11. Experimenting
12. Defining operationally
13. Formulating models
14. Interpreting data

Next, I looked at a paper, "Outcomes of Inquiry-Based Science Education" (Schindel 1991), distributed at an ESIP meeting. Dr. Schindel stressed that the list was that of one scientist and not from a group or organization, but

I thought that I could learn from one scientist as well as I could from a host of scientists. The paper from Dr. Schindel fit into my plan, so I used it, too.

Outcomes of Inquiry-Based Science Education

Children should:
- Believe that their observations have standing that can compete with the written word.
- Be able to explain their understandings of ideas and defend them against alternatives.
- Be able to translate an observation into useable data.
- Be able to marshal data into predictions.
- Modify individual concepts based on new data.
- Identify gaps in their understanding and pose questions to fill them in.
- Be disturbed by incongruent observations.
- Be able to recognize patterns in data in order to limit observations.
- Be able to recognize alternative explanations for observations.
- Be able to pose effective questions and design fair tests to distinguish between alternatives.
- Be able to persuade others that their observations, procedures, and explanations are valid.
- Be able to determine which course of action—collecting data, thinking about data, formulating an explanation, or asking about a new question—should come next.

My next source of information was Dr. Joe Griffith (pers. com. 1991), the project director for Science and Technology for Children (STC), a school curriculum project being developed by the National Science Resources Center. As Dr. Griffith pointed out in our conversation, his list of equipment and his list of ways to communicate—see below—are intended to be examples.

STC Process Skills

OBSERVE
    Making observations
    Selecting observations for further study

USE PATTERNS
    Seeking and identifying patterns
    Suggesting and evaluating explanations of patterns
COMMUNICATE
    Speaking, writing, sketching, graphing
HANDLE EQUIPMENT
    Using rulers, thermometers, balances, screwdrivers, pliers
DESIGN AND CARRY OUT EXPERIMENTS
BRING KNOWLEDGE TO BEAR IN SOLVING PROBLEMS
    Asking questions
    Wondering

How to Think like a Scientist: Answering Questions by the Scientific Method (Kramer 1987), a children's book, gave me this:

> These five steps are called the scientific method:
> 1. Ask a question.
> 2. Gather information about the question.
> 3. Form a hypothesis.
> 4. Test the hypothesis.
> 5. Tell others what you found.

My final source of information was the Fairfax County Public Schools (FCPS), Virginia, *Program of Studies* (1989). There were no lists of process skills, but there was some interesting information on the "Science" page in the "Subject Overviews" section:

> Each unit is designed to encourage children to investigate the nature of the world around them by carrying out their own experiments. Through this process children acquire much useful information, not by rote, but through their own active involvement in problem-solving activities. This kind of active learning experience emphasizes, even to the very young student, the essence of science—open inquiry combined with experimentation. Five basic developmental goals are common to the program: curiosity and interest, initiative and inventiveness, observation and record keeping, independent critical thinking, and persistence. (SO.21)

In these documents, I began to see patterns of phrases and ideas. I discussed my thinking with several friends, and I asked myself questions. Suddenly, in a glorious moment of discovery and revelation, I realized that I was doing it. I was doing science! In my search for the scientific method, I had collected information, looked for patterns, posed questions, made a connection with what I knew about language processes, and communicated my ideas to friends.

I wondered why some folks seemed to insist that there was one list of science process skills and why they defended the need for one list; I questioned how different learning styles fit with this all-purpose, definitive list; and eventually I answered my question in a way that made sense to me. I concluded that there was no single, definitive list to describe science process and that there was no need for one, as long as the stated processes supported discovering, understanding, making sense of the world, and solving problems. It sounded so simple in retrospect, but I knew that it represented a lot of hard work.

I returned to the familiar, whole language, and decided that I needed to reaffirm what I knew about language process. I reread parts of *In the Middle: Writing, Reading, and Learning with Adolescents* (Atwell 1987), *Writing: Teachers and Children at Work* (Graves 1983), and *Workshop 1: Writing and Literature* (Atwell 1989). As I read about Jeremy in Karen Weinhold's "Process and Empowerment," the last article in *Workshop 1*, I was struck again by what happens to learners in process classrooms: learners have the time to pursue a topic of personal interest, have real opportunities to make decisions and choices, receive feedback from their peers and teacher, engage in ongoing self-evaluation, and are valued and respected members of a community of learners. Not only had I observed this as a teacher, but also I had experienced it as a learner and had wallowed in that sweet feeling of success.

What would happen, I suddenly wondered, if I substituted "science" for "language" in thinking about my students? Would my description of learners in a language process classroom apply to learners in a science process classroom? I thought about the science program in my classroom. In the early 1970s, my school system had adopted a series of hands-on, inquiry-based science units for the elementary grades. Grades 2–6 received four unit kits during the school year, and each kit contained a well-written and helpful teacher's manual, student activities booklets, and all of the necessary equipment for the scientific investigations and experiments. (Grade 1 received one kit, which focused on nature and was a year-long study.)

The Fairfax County program did not require me to be a dispenser of facts or the voice of authority, so my personal fear of science did not inhibit science learning in the classroom. Actually, my insecurity may have fostered the learning because I participated in the experiments and activities along with the children. I was as much a student as any of the children, and they were very accepting and encouraging as we posed questions, designed experiments, shared observations, recorded information, and learned from one another. Those students were making decisions, giving and receiving feedback, evaluating themselves, and building a community of learners.

The biggest difference between language and science studies in my classroom involved the pursuit of a topic of personal interest. In language, the children selected their own trade books and their own writing topics, but in science, the unit of study generally was predetermined. Although the formal study of science focused on preselected topics, there were opportunities for students to pursue their own interests and to work independently. In addition to the science kits, each classroom received a collection of science trade books for students to use as resources or as extensions of personal interest. Activity cards also were developed for each book.

Looking at my students helped me realize that in a process classroom, regardless of curricular subject, each person's thoughts are valued and respected, leading each person to develop a sense of power and positive self-esteem. As I continued to think about children and science, I experienced one of those grand "aha" moments in learning. I suddenly understood the difference between science process and process science, and it made great sense. I defined science process as the procedure that a person goes through in looking for an answer or in seeking information about a science question. The procedure is not fixed in order, is not a recipe, and is not linear. Instead, it is recursive, is not always observable (parts of the process are mental), and includes behaviors that are implied or stated. Process science is hands-on, inquiry-based science in the pursuit of which students have the time and opportunity to use science processes. The scientific method issue became confusing for people like me because it crossed process science and science process.

Finally, I felt ready to look at the question of how to assess and evaluate science, using what I knew about whole language assessment and evaluation.

Purpose of Assessment and Evaluation

Routman (1991) describes the difference between assessment and evaluation: " 'Assessment' refers to data collection and the gathering of evidence. 'Evaluation' implies bringing meaning to that data through interpretation, analysis, and reflection and includes the kinds of instructional decisions that are made by careful examination of the evidence." (302) And it now generally is understood (see Harp 1991, 35–36, among others) that the purpose of assessing and evaluating is to construct a history of the learner's development in order to help:

1. The student see and understand his or her progress and make self-evaluations.
2. The teacher make instructional decisions and make self-evaluations.
3. The parents, administrators, and other teachers see and understand the student's progress.
4. Adults outside the local community see and understand the student's progress.

From a teacher's perspective, it was vital that the student be included in the assessment and evaluation process. The teacher provides time, opportunity, and support for each student to move toward self-evaluation, because self-evaluation is one strategy that helps children become independent learners. It also was necessary for me to include teacher self-evaluation as one of the purposes of assessment and evaluation. During the last ten years, I have realized that when a lesson "bombs" or when my students are having difficulty academically, I need to examine my teaching instead of labeling the students as lazy or incapable or one of those other negative words that excuses me from providing meaningful instruction. Parents needed to be included because of their personal interests in receiving information about their children's learning.

There are more global reasons for the local school administrator to look at the learning of students. In my experience, the principal used the assessment and evaluation data to look for patterns of progress, to identify needs based on feedback from all school personnel, and to set schoolwide goals and work plans. Other teacher specialists used these patterns of development to assist teachers with instructional design. I included administrators outside the local school community—central office administrators and local, state, and national legislators—to address professional and political realities. Also, I believed this group needed to be reeducated to see the broader picture of assessment and evaluation instead of to rely on standardized test scores.

Assessment and Evaluation Strategies and Instruments

I next looked at the assessment and evaluation strategies and instruments used in whole language, with an eye toward using or adapting them in science. After looking at forty to fifty different strategies and instruments, I finally decided to stick with the ones that I used in my classroom because I valued what they enabled me to see.

The assessment and evaluation strategies and instruments that I use can be separated into seven categories: (1) activity records, (2) anecdotal records, (3) checklists, (4) interviews and questionnaires, (5) journals and logs, (6) portfolios, and (7) reading/writing folders. There are several factors that determine which strategy or instrument I use at a given moment: What do I want to find out? What is the most efficient way to do so? How do I want to report my findings?

Activity Records

Activity records, which provide a quick check on how time is used in class, enable students to evaluate their work and me to make instructional decisions. Most of my activity records were adapted from Nancie Atwell's *In The Middle* (1987), the single most useful and practical language-process book I have read. (Blank forms for the records discussed here are included in the Appendix to this chapter. They are suitable for you to reproduce and you may feel free to do so.)

"Status of the Class" (Figure 5–1) is the simplest way to keep track of the students' daily activities. At the beginning of each writing workshop, I spend three to five minutes recording what each student plans to do. As I call the students' names, they tell me the title of their piece and their plans for working on that piece, and I fill in the information in a blank space next to their name. Having that information for the whole class enables me to identify, for example, which students are not having conferences or sharing their writing with the whole class, and I plan mini-lessons accordingly.

STATUS OF THE CLASS

	MONDAY	TUESDAY	WEDNESDAY	THURSDAY	FRIDAY
Rachel			10/2 ACT 3 ·Heaping WC (ACT 2)	10/3 RI GC	WC (ACT 3) SN Collected RB Make A Splash
Tina			ACT 2 PC WC (ACT 2)	RI GC ACT 3	WC (ACT 3) SN -Collected RB Water and Life
Pam			ACT 3 WC (ACT 2)	ACT 3 RI PC GC	WC (ACT 3) SN -Collected ACT. 4 ·Surface Tension
Travis			ACT 3 WC (ACT 2)	ACT 3 RI PC	WC (ACT 3) SN - Collected EA - Heaping drops of other liquids
Tyler			EA - Racing drops of other liquids WC (ACT 2)	GC about liquid races ACT 3	WC (ACT 3) SN -Collected ACT. 4

ACT # - Activity and its number   PC - Conference with partner

RI - Recording Information   GC - Group Conference

SN - Science Notebook   WC - Whole Class Discussion

EA - Extension Activity   RB - Reading a book on science topic

FIGURE 5–1. Looking at this class status form, I realize that students are not recording information as they work on an activity but are waiting until the activity is completed. We need to review the importance of collecting written data at every step of an experiment.

At the beginning of reading workshop, I do the same roll call, and the students, one by one, tell me their plans for the day. Additionally, each student (or pair of students) has an individual status sheet (Figure 5–2). At a glance, students can see how they are spending their time and the progress they are making on some activities.

In adapting Atwell's reading and writing forms so that I could use them in science, I realized that the framework could remain constant although the content would differ. The simple and flexible format enabled my class and me to record our daily activities.

STATUS OF Rachel K. - Katra

DATE	MONDAY	TUESDAY	WEDNESDAY	THURSDAY	FRIDAY
Week of 10/1	✗	NO Science	Act 3-heaping WC	RI GC	WC SN RB make a splash
Week of 10/7	Act4 Surface tension RI PC	SN WC Act4 Quiz	Act5 soap & water RI PC	NO Science	SN EA Study new vocabulary
Week of 10/14	WC Act 6 Act F Using the Balence	Act6 RI PC GC	NO Science	Act7 mesuring forces	Act7 Mesuring forces
Week of 10/21	EA Washers to see how long for Plastic 3	Graph SN GC	Act8 mass Layering RI	NO Science	PC RI Sumery sheet GC
Week of 10/28	NO Science	WC Science vocabulary	Act 9 Charecteristic of state of matter	Act 9 PC RI Act 9 WC	

ACT # - Activity and its number

RI - Recording Information

SN - Science Notebook

EA - Extension Activity

PC - Conference with partner

GC - Group Conference

WC - Whole Class Discussion

RB - Reading a book on science topic

FIGURE 5–2. According to this individual status record, these two students spend about half their class time on hands-on activities. I need to find out if that is enough time for them to complete each experiment, observing and understanding everything that happened.

Anecdotal Records

Anecdotal records are informal, written documentation of what the teacher observes a student or group of students doing; they have been very helpful in both reading and writing workshop. I record students' questions, discussion comments, time on-task, and other observable behaviors, concentrating on positive performance and avoiding subjective interpretations of behavior.

At individual conferences, I use the anecdotal records to help students focus on documented behavior. Because I maintain an objective stance, students often feel encouraged to make decisions about changing or modifying their behaviors. Self-evaluations have led students to speak up more often in discussion groups, to make sure that everyone has the opportunity to talk, to increase their time on-task, or to make encouraging comments to classmates. Self-evaluations clearly are more powerful for some students than teacher evaluations.

I write my notes on a form (a simple rectangular box—see Figure 5–3) I developed through trial and error, but other teachers use computer labels or stick-on notes. Early in September, I make master copies of the form, listing students alphabetically by last name, and then make photocopies throughout the year as I need them. The space at the top is filled in with helpful information such as date, time, and activity. I use different colored pens so that I can track which subject I'm referring to. When my notes fill the rectangles, I cut them out and tape each one onto a piece of notebook paper with the student's name at the top. These notes are kept in a three-ring binder, and I add more sheets as needed during the year. I try to observe each child at least once a week, even if it is for only five minutes.

Sometimes I write anecdotal records immediately after a large-group or whole-class discussion. Last year, for instance, one of the books that I read aloud to my class was *A Snake-Lover's Diary* (Brenner 1970). Students initiated a discussion as soon as I finished reading the last page. The resulting anecdotal record (Figure 5–4) gave me information to pursue in later small-group or individual conferences. For example, I wanted to know more about Geoffrey's and Joshua's reading for information about a topic of interest; I wanted to find out if Chad frequently used "me" for "I"; and I wanted to see if Justin ate that hot dog! Also I wanted to find out which students talked in small-group discussions but not in large groups and which students never or seldom talked, regardless of group size. In other words, some of my anecdotal records document questions that refer to science content, some to science process, and some to other areas of the curriculum.

Checklists

Examining my reading and writing checklists, I discovered that I use them as visual reminders for my students and me, in much the same way that forgetful people rely on lists when grocery shopping or running errands.

Barbara - 11/15 - Science: B. and partner predicted paper clip would sink; when clip floated, they decided it was because clip was not wet; they predicted wet clip would sink in water but did not try it; wrote in their notes "Surface tension is an object that is not wet on top."

Barbara - 11/19 - Science: B. and partner worked with J. and D. on paper clip experiment; J. pointed out that wet clip floated as well as dry clip in plain water and both sank in soapy water; B- "I just don't get this. Why does it float when it's wet and when it's dry? It must be the soapy water, but what is surface tension anyway?"; all 4 decided to continue meeting on 11/20.

FIGURE 5–3. These anecdotal records offer evidence that this student devised a hypothesis unsupported by evidence and later was disturbed when confronted with evidence that conflicted with her hypothesis. She recognized that soap had an effect on water and identified her question for further study.

These checklists remind us of certain writing conventions, of helpful reading and writing strategies, and of requirements for projects or final products. Usually, I hook the students with a simple question (What do you do in reading when you come to a word that you don't know?) and their responses become a checklist.

3/15/91 - 11:15 A.M. - <u>Snake-Lover's Diary</u> discussion

Heather: Why did boy decide to give mom iguana. "Why did he choose iguana over other lizards?"

Me: I don't know. Maybe iguana interested him more than other lizards.

Barbara: Friend has iguana. "You would not believe how huge it is!"

Janot: "Is there a sequel about the boy's study of lizards?"

Me: I don't know. <u>Snake...</u> published in 1970 so plenty of time to write sequel. Maybe someone who goes to library after lunch could try to find out.

Geoffrey: I found painted turtle in Nov. and kept it at my house through winter. "I read about painted turtles and found out that scientists discovered in 1975 that painted turtles carry a bacteria that causes humans to become very ill." Since then, pet stores have been banned from selling painted turtles. G. has some concerns about the bacteria but doesn't want to release turtle until weather warms up. Handles turtle very little.

Joshua: Read that any foreign "permanent material put on a turtle's shell cause great irritation" to the turtle and is a "cruel thing to do."

Justin: When visiting Grandmother in Florida, J. left table for a moment and returned to find a "small lizard sitting on my hot dog!"

Chad: "My grandmother lives in Florida, too, and there are chameleons outside close to her condo. Me and my brother always try to catch them, but we never get any. They move too fast."

(Had to stop to go to lunch.)

FIGURE 5-4. Another form of anecdotal record. Geoffrey's comments show how a student's personal interest motivates him to find out more information about the topic.

For example, the second week of school, students were asked to tell me what they really, truly, honestly, for sure and certain knew about writing conventions to use in every written assignment, in every story, in every piece of writing that they did this year. Before students declare a piece "finished," they check this list. I also use it to keep track of each student's consistent ability to apply the skills. New skills are added to individuals' checklists as needed.

A similar question (What are some things that are important to do in science that you already know how to do?) started the students thinking about and identifying skills and strategies to use during science. We first listed everyone's suggestions and then negotiated to devise a slightly more concise list (Figure 5–5). All the students approved this list, which one named "Science Know-Hows."

The students decided that Science Know-Hows would be more useful as a wall chart to refer to while engaged in science activities and experiments than as a notebook checklist. Their working checklists are unit specific and are used for self-evaluations (Figure 5–6) and to assess and evaluate their science notebooks (Figure 5–7).

Interviews and Questionnaires

I use interviews and questionnaires to ask explicit questions that narrow the scope of information, take little of my time in class, and provide me with immediate, written evidence to assess and evaluate outside class time. Often students are asked to fill out the forms prior to the interviews, and I use the interview time to make certain that we both understand their written responses.

Early each school year, I want to know how the students view themselves in connection with reading and writing, so, borrowing from Nancie Atwell (1987), I administer a reading survey and a writing survey. Recognizing the value of that data, I adapted the surveys to gather information about science (Figure 5–8).

Responses to the surveys give me information about attitudes, experiences, conceptions, and levels of involvement. The surveys are filed in a three-ring binder for the students and me to review at least quarterly when writing personal reading and writing goals. The quarterly goals are part of another form that I borrowed from Atwell and adapted.

In a quarterly letter, students evaluate their reading and writing development, and a follow-up interview allows time for me to plan goals for

Read and understand directions before you experiment.						
Get all materials.						
Carefully follow directions.						
Be patient and persistent.						
Observe everything that happens.						
Take precise, neat notes.						
Repeat the experiment if you don't understand what happens.						
Ask questions.						
Help other people.						
Cooperate with your partner.						
Be serious with your experiments.						
Work neatly and carefully.						
Use the proper equipment.						
Use equipment safely.						
Take care of the equipment.						
Measure very carefully.						
If you are curious, try some experiments even if they're not in the booklet.						
Think before writing the answer to a question.						
Answer all questions.						
Write neatly and explain everything completely.						
Label your drawings, graphs, and charts.						
Clean up after yourself.						

FIGURE 5–5. This checklist reflects the order in which suggestions were made by students. It would be interesting to ask students to rewrite the list grouping skills and strategies.

Self Evaluation Sheet for
Investigating Matter: Liquids

Required Content
I answered all questions in:
___✓ Act. A   ___✓ Act. B   ___✓ Act. C
___✓ Act. D   ___✓ Act. E   ___✓ Act. F
___✓ Act. G   ___✓ Act. H   ___✓ Act. I
___✓ Act. J   ___✓ Act. K   ___✓ Act. L

I labeled all:
___✓ pictures   ___✓ charts   ___✓ graphs

I defined all terms in my own words:
___✓ Vocabulary for Act. A - E
___✓ Vocabulary for Act. F - I
___✓ Vocabulary for Act. J - L

I completed all quizzes:
___✓ Quiz 1   ___✓ Quiz 2   ___✓ Quiz 3

Extra Content

___✓ I did extra investigations
My question: Is the surface tension of glycerin the
             same as water?
My prediction: Glycerin has more surface tension
My experiment: Put plastic plates on glycerin and counted the
My observations: number of paper clips to pull it off.
             It took more paper clips -38
My explanations: Glycerine has stronger surface tension because
Conventions   its more cohesive

___✓ I followed "Conventions for All
      Written Work."
___✓ I observed "Science Know-Hows."

Extensions

Questions I still have that are
related to this unit:
   How do scientists see small molecules
      of something?

**FIGURE 5–6. This kind of self-evaluation form gives students an overview
of the requirements for a unit and provides a way for students to keep track
of what they need to do.**

and with the student. The letters also give me topics for future minilessons
and provide data for evaluating past minilessons. I now use a quarterly
letter in science as well (Figure 5–9). Through this process, students bring
that same metacognitive sophistication to science that once was reserved
only for language arts.

Notebook Requirements for
Investigating Matter: Liquids

✓ Act. A - describe appearance of drops
of water, glycerin, alcohol; describe
behaviors of the liquids when like
drops get too close; compare the liquids

✓ Act. B - explain and describe cohesion
and adhesion as observed in activity A

✓ Act. C - relate heaping ability and drop
size of the three liquids to cohesion

✓ Quiz 1

✓ Act. D - describe surface tension

✓ Act. E - investigate and describe effects
of soap on water's cohesive force and
surface tension

✓ Vocab., Act. A - E, -use own words to
define terms related to liquids

✓ Act. F - assemble the balance; practice
using the balance

✓ Act. G - investigate cohesive and
adhesive forces of four liquids; record
data on chart and create a graph

✓ Act. H - weigh three liquids; record data
predict layering of liquids; experiment
to check predictions

✓ Act. I - summarize data from Act. A -I
using comparison chart; look for patterns
and make generalizations about liquids

✓ Vocab., Act. F - I (same as above Vocab)

✓ Quiz 2

✓ Act. J - compare solids, liquids, gases;
use chart to organize comparisons;
identify heat as a catalyst

✓ Act. K - control variables and compare
melting times of ice cubes in different
amounts of water and air; record data on
chart and graph; describe and explain

✓ Act. L - investigate insulating
qualities of materials; record data
on chart and graph

✓ Vocab., Act. J - L

✓ Quiz 3

FIGURE 5–7. Students use this checklist to ensure that their notebooks are complete. When I check notebooks, I use the list to keep track of the contents of each student's notebook, underlining or circling missing information.

Jeffrey Goodall 'S SCIENCE SURVEY

1. Are you a scientist? _no_ (If your response is "yes," answer question 2a. If your response is "no," answer question 2b.)

2a. How did you learn how to do science (observe, experiment, collect data, etc.)?

_____

_____

2b. How do people learn how to do science (observe, experiment, collect data, etc.)? _They experiment and observe and they take notes._

3. Why do people do science? _I think some do it for fun and some do it to help the world._

4. What do you think a person needs to do in order to be a good scientist? _I think a person would need to have good tools._

5. How does your teacher decide which students are good scientists? _They are serious about it and work hard._

6. What do you like to do in science? _I like to do experiments but I don't like to write notes._

7. What kinds of science experiences have you had outside of school? _Just little things from my science kit._

8. Do you know the names of any scientists? List as many as you can remember. _Albert Einstein, Alexander Grahm Bell, Thomas Edison_

9. In general, how do you feel about science? _1-10 I rate it a 4._

FIGURE 5–8. This student's science survey suggests that he lacks an understanding of the value of notes for his personal use in science. I need to plan several minilessons to address that need, illustrating and/or discussing the many uses of written data in science.

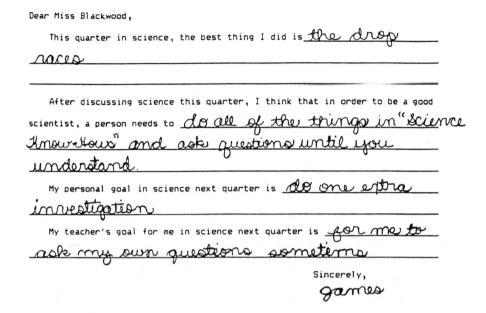

Dear Miss Blackwood,

This quarter in science, the best thing I did is *the drop races*

After discussing science this quarter, I think that in order to be a good scientist, a person needs to *do all of the things in "science Know-How" and ask questions until you understand.*

My personal goal in science next quarter is *do one extra investigation*

My teacher's goal for me in science next quarter is *for me to ask my own questions sometimes*

Sincerely,
James

FIGURE 5–9. In his quarterly letter, this student, on his own, identified "asking questions" as important in science. That may give him some feeling of ownership in the goal that I have for him.

Journals and Logs

In my sixth-grade classroom, students write personal responses to the books they are reading or to the books that I read aloud. Each student has a spiral notebook that serves as a dialogue journal, and the journal entries are written as friendly letters. The students begin with letters only to me but eventually write to their friends, and every letter receives a reply. The letters are drafts and are not corrected or graded.

There are some requirements, and when those requirements are not met, I point this out in my written replies to students. Writing a personal response to a book is challenging for some students, but I remain firm about that expectation and spend considerable time explaining and modeling written personal responses. I do not accept book reviews, book reports, or story retelling. I explain to the students that our letters are a cycle: the first step is the student's personal response to the book; my personal response to the student's journal entry is the second step; and at step three, the student writes a personal response either to my letter or to the book. I compare our letters to a dance, with the student's leading and my following and our needing to work together in order to be successful. Over the last three years, I danced smoothly and successfully with seventy-eight students (out of a total of eighty), stepping on just a few toes in the process.

Although dialogue journals take a tremendous amount of my time, they are my favorite assessment and evaluation tool. Through the letters I get to know my students as people and quickly learn to appreciate their knowledge and experiences.

When the students write to each other they use less formal language, but the quality of the responses does not decline.

One dialogue journal per student is as much as I could handle, so I decided to combine science trade books and the reading response journals by encouraging students to write personal response letters to science books that they read or that I read aloud. I was a little anxious about the merger, but my students jumped right in and showed me that natural curiosity about science does lead to personal responses to science trade books.

In journals, students choose the topic about which to write. In logs, the students write about a topic selected by me, by another student, or by a group of students. I use logs to elicit timely self-evaluations by students, for their evaluations of a lesson, for their suggestions about a class problem, for their questions on a particular subject, for their explanations of a concept recently taught, and for a variety of other information. When I read their logs, I am able to evaluate my teaching and to make instructional decisions based on their input. I usually do not write in students' logs.

Recently, after our first experiments with liquids, I asked the students to respond to this question: "What do you think about some of the activities that you and your science partner did?" Here are some of their responses:

> My first reaction to the first science that we did was "can I do it?" I wasn't sure what was going to happen, the science wasn't that hard. I've never [worked] with glycerin before.

> Surprisingly enough, I actually enjoyed science today. It's really interesting. You see, I've always hated, just hated science. Now here I am enjoying it! Weird! Taneka is a real great partner to have.

> Our first experience in science was a pleasant one. It was a time to experiment with liquids and to see how glycerin tastes (just kidding). I think we did a good job.

In science I had a great time. It was fun, and the glycerin was very sticky. The alcohol didn't even pile up.

I encourage my students to evaluate themselves in both their journals and their logs, suggesting that they begin with a self-compliment and then identify one or two areas where improvement is needed; thus they design a plan to address those needs. I believe that self-evaluation leads to self-reliance and to independence, and I nudge my students, frequently, in that direction.

Portfolios

The archival nature of portfolios makes them a logical place to save examples of a student's work over a period of one or more years. Work samples are either student selected or teacher selected. Attached to each sample is an index card on which the student or teacher explains the reasons for choosing that particular piece of work. After introducing the mechanics and purposes of portfolios, the teacher collaborates with the students to determine the appropriate number of samples to be collected each quarter.

Toward the end of each grading period, the teacher schedules individual conferences to discuss the contents of each student's portfolio and to evaluate progress as shown by the selections. To encourage self-evaluation, students are asked to identify areas of growth and to share their opinions about why and how that improvement occurred. The contents of the portfolio should provide evidence of the student's progress and of the learning process.

Reading/Writing Folders

Reading/writing folders hold students' works in progress, display helpful information relating to daily reading and writing, and provide space to record additional data that may be useful in reading and writing activities. My students use folders that were developed and published by Fairfax County Public Schools; the folders are very convenient for storing and retrieving both papers and information. The folders open into three full sections, each with an inside pocket to hold papers. Each pocket or flap displays ideas or strategies to help students plan for reading and writing. There is space for students to list information about their pieces of writing and about the works of professional authors. The information is presented in a useful, nonthreatening format, and the folder's design promotes self-evaluation.

Using the reading and writing folder as a model for creating a science folder seemed a natural next step, but it proved to be more difficult than I had anticipated. I continue to collaborate with my colleague JoAnn DeMaria to develop one that is both useful and practical.

What About Standardized Tests?

I purposefully excluded standardized tests from my list of assessment and evaluation strategies and instruments. Years ago, I realized that standardized test scores did not help me assess and evaluate students, did not help students evaluate themselves, and, from the perspective of the classroom teacher, did not deserve the importance attached to them.

Across the country, tremendous resources are devoted to test preparation, administration, and interpretation; test results are used to judge the success or failure of students, teachers, administrators, schools, and systems. At the same time, many teachers and students are engaged in problem-solving activities in classrooms where process is as important as product, where students are respected and valued as thinking individuals, where continuous evaluation directs teaching and learning. Multiple-choice tests are at odds with the move toward process classrooms and with the call from business leaders to strengthen students' problem-solving abilities and cooperative skills.

Not the End

As I reviewed the assessment and evaluation strategies and instruments used by my students and me, I thought of the time, decisions, and revisions involved in selecting those strategies and instruments. I am impressed with us, but I realize that we aren't finished. We face the ongoing task that all teachers and their students face: making decisions about which tools are most effective and efficient for our purposes. As the teacher, I need to guide the selection process and, at the same time, to include the students in a realistic and meaningful way. I also need to continue learning about assessment and evaluation.

As this preliminary comparison of assessment and evaluation in whole language and science neared an end, I concluded that the real connection was process. When the emphasis is on the process of learning, not on the product, strategies and techniques are applicable across the curriculum. The strategies and techniques can be for assessing and evaluating, or for teaching and learning, or for problem solving. And I offer this cautionary advice: These assessment procedures represent ten years of refining, adapting, and phasing in ideas that work for me and my students. Attempts to use too many instruments too quickly may be frustrating and burdensome. So be selective, and start slowly.

I began with the question, How can I use what I know about whole language assessment and evaluation to assess and evaluate science? In the exploration of that topic, other questions surfaced, and some remain unanswered. I still wonder about ways to incorporate topic choice into a prescribed curriculum without manipulating either the students or the curriculum. I wonder if it is possible to have a truly integrated day with no blocks of time reserved for science and math and social studies. I wonder if I'll always have more questions than answers.

I hope that the answer to the last question is yes.

References

Atwell, N. 1987. In the middle: Writing, reading, and learning with adolescents. Portsmouth, N.H.: Boynton/Cook.

———, ed. 1989. *Workshop 1: Writing and literature*. Workshop by and for Teachers. Portsmouth, N.H.: Heinemann.

———, ed. 1990. *Coming to know: Writing to learn in the intermediate grades*. Portsmouth, N.H.: Heinemann.

Au, K., J. Scheu, A. Kawakami, and P. Herman. 1990. Assessment and accountability in a whole literacy curriculum. *The Reading Teacher* (April): 574–78.

Bradford, J. K. 1987. Making language arts creative. *The School Administrator* (November): 15–16.

Brenner, B. 1970. *A snake-lover's diary*. New York: Harper and Row.

Clem, C., and K. Feathers. 1986. I lic spidrs: What one child teaches us about content learning. *Language Arts* (February): 143–47.

Fairfax County Public Schools. 1989. *Elementary program of studies: kindergarten through grade six.* Fairfax, Va.: Office of Curriculum Services, Department of Instructional Services.

Fillion, B. 1983. Let me see you learn. *Language Arts* (September): 702–10.

Graves, D. 1983. *Writing: Teachers and children at work.* Portsmouth, N.H.: Heinemann.

Harp, B., ed. 1991. *Assessment and evaluation in whole language programs.* Norwood, Mass.: Christopher Gordon.

Johnston, P. 1987. Teachers as evaluation experts. *The Reading Teacher* (April): 744–48.

Kramer, S. 1987. *How to think like a scientist: Answering questions by the scientific method.* New York: Crowell.

Manning, M., and G. Manning. 1991. Time for reflection and growth. *Teaching K–8* (May): 98–100.

Rakow, S. 1986. *Teaching science as inquiry.* Bloomington, Ind.: Phi Delta Kappa Educational Foundation.

Reardon, S. J. 1990. Putting reading tests in their place. *The New Advocate* (Winter): 29–37.

Rief, L. 1990. Finding value in evaluation: Self-assessment in a middle school classroom. *Educational Leadership* (March): 24–29.

Routman, R. 1991. *Invitations: Changing as teachers and learners K–12.* Portsmouth, N.H.: Heinemann.

Schindel, D. 1991. Outcomes of inquiry-based science education. Paper presented at Elementary Science Integration Project Summer Workshop, June 27.

Siu-Runyan, Y. 1990. Begin your teaching by observing. *The Colorado Communicator* (November): 24–29.

Teale, W., E. Hiebert, and E. Chittenden. 1987. Assessing young children's literacy development. *The Reading Teacher* (April): 772–77.

Valencia, S., and D. Pearson. 1987. Reading assessment: Time for a change. *The Reading Teacher* (April): 726–32.

Appendix 5–1
Reproducible Forms

STATUS OF THE CLASS

Student	MONDAY	TUESDAY	WEDNESDAY	THURSDAY	FRIDAY

ACT #—Activity and its number　　PC—Conference with Partner
RI—Recording Information　　　　GC—Group Conference
SN—Science Notebook　　　　　　WC—Whole-Class Discussion
EA—Extension Activity　　　　　　RB—Reading Book (on science topic)

Adapted, with permission of the author and publisher, from Nancie Atwell, *In the Middle: Writing, Reading, and Learning with Adolescents*. (Portsmouth, NH: Boynton/Cook Publishers, 1987), 91.

STATUS OF _____

Date	MONDAY	TUESDAY	WEDNESDAY	THURSDAY	FRIDAY

ACT #—Activity and its number   PC—Conference with Partner
RI—Recording Information   GC—Group Conference
SN—Science Notebook   WC—Whole-Class Discussion
EA—Extension Activity   RB—Reading Book (on science topic)

Adapted, with permission of the author and publisher, from Nancie Atwell, *In the Middle: Writing, Reading, and Learning with Adolescents*. (Portsmouth, NH: Boynton/Cook Publishers, 1987), 91.

_____'S SCIENCE SURVEY

1.   Are you a scientist? _____ (If your response is "yes," answer

question 2a. If your response is "no," answer question 2b.)

2a.   How did you learn how to do science (observe, experiment, collect

data, etc.)? _____

_____

2b.   How do people learn how to do science (observe, experiment, collect

data, etc.)?_____

_____

3.   Why do people do science?_____

_____

4.   What do you think a person needs to do in order to be a good

scientist?_____

_____

5.   How does your teacher decide which students are good scientists?___

_____

6.   What do you like to do in science?_____

_____

7.   What kinds of science experiences have you had outside school?_____

_____

8.   Do you know the names of any scientists? List as many as you can

remember._____

9.   In general, how do you feel about science?_____

_____

Adapted, with permission of the author and publisher, from Nancie Atwell, *In the Middle: Writing, Reading, and Learning with Adolescents.* (Portsmouth, NH: Boynton/Cook Publishers, 1987), 270–72.

Dear Miss Blackwood,

    This quarter in science, the best thing I did is _____

_____

_____.

    After discussing science this quarter, I think that in order to be a
good scientist, a person needs to _____

_____

_____.

    My personal goal in science next quarter is _____

_____.

    My teacher's goal for me in science next quarter is _____

_____.

                                       Sincerely,

6 Mary Dickinson Bird

The Stuff of Science Workshop: A Sampler of Materials and Resources

How It Began

"But Ms. B., how does the sun get into the earth?"

It was the voice of Glenn, a feisty, low-achieving second grader, whose question brought an abrupt halt to the class discussion of moon observations. In the silence that followed, I wondered with mingled anxiety, chagrin, and exhilaration what Glenn was really asking and why. After all, we were simply debating whether the moon last night had been a backward C or a frontward C; no one had mentioned the sun at all. Nevertheless, I decided to risk fishing for what might turn out to be red herring. I invited Glenn to elaborate on his question.

Did I say red herring? In fact, Glenn's outburst led the class to reel in a giant, tentacled monster that soon became our class mascot! With a seemingly unrelated question, Glenn had launched us all on a year-long study of the fascinating connections among light, heat, electricity, measurement, energy conservation, ecosystems, optics, and mythology.

Here's how it happened. Glenn had remembered, from some independent reading (this, from a student considered barely able to read, and certainly not "independently") that the moon's light is really reflected sunlight. He remembered, too, that the sun warms the earth. His question, when he'd fully explained it, was actually an array of wonderings. Glenn was asking about reflections; the comparative warmth of sunlight and moonlight; the connections between light and dark; the relationship between heat and light; the production, transfer, and measurement of energy; and the impact of energy on our world. Given the opportunity to articulate his curiosities, Glenn got the whole class wondering with him, and looking to me, their science teacher, for guidance.

Like any teacher, I had a few questions of my own. Where should we begin our new investigations? How would these explorations fit in with the city science curriculum for second grade? Did it matter (did I care?) if investigations took us outside the boundaries of curriculum? How much did I know about these topics? How much did I need to know? What could I do to learn more? And where would I find the resources to empower my students to follow through on their fascinating questions and take their science learning into their own hands?

Throughout my years as a science resource teacher for one of Boston's elementary schools and now as I work primarily with teachers, these questions were and are the backdrop against which students' science investigations are carried out. They are the questions that shaped my goal — not to provide a cookbook for child-centered science instruction but to offer ideas and support to teachers who are eager to let curiosity and passion drive classroom activities.

Where the Ideas Came From

The topics included in this resource guide will seem familiar in some cases, quirky in others, because they are an authentic catalog of investigations that my students, kindergarten through grade six, pursued over the course of several years. In some cases, the curriculum was the starting point. For example, haven't most of us done "sink or float" units in the primary grades? We just don't usually follow it up, as my kids decided to do, with a trip to the local marina to inspect the drafts of real boats, or with a detailed study of diving mechanisms in whales.

In other cases, as in the one that opened this chapter, student explorations were prompted by questions that steered us away from traditional curriculum but much deeper into understanding of phenomena. Glenn and his second-grade classmates might have had trouble listing the planets in order, but they acquired an understanding of conduction and convection that was more sophisticated than that of most college students. That understanding contributed significantly to their subsequent grasp of meteorology, ecology, and energy conservation.

A few of these investigations arose, I admit, as a result of my own interests and curiosities. All of us have some special skill or knowledge that can help open up the world to our students. For me it was marine biology and textile arts; for you it might be cooking, aviation, or folktales. In any case, it's easy to be imaginative about investigations of a subject we know and love, and it's exciting to find our own passions contributing to—and benefiting from—our students' curiosity and growth. When you have the additional opportunity, as I sometimes did, of teaming with a colleague who has complementary interests, the potential for expanding children's experience and building on their questions is enormous.

Where Ideas Can Take You

The samples that follow are only a few of the science explorations my students and I pursued.

They represent a kind of roughly penciled map of the routes my students and I traveled in search of materials and information for science investigations. The questions that were raised; the equipment and supplies we found useful; the people, places, and reference materials that helped us—all are offered in the hope that they will invite you and your students to join the expedition into the rich experience of science, discovering your own pathways to understanding.

As you will see, there *are* myriad pathways through the thicket of scientific investigation. The resources and ideas the remainder of this chapter describes arose out of a specific set of circumstances. The route you and your students choose, and the map you make together, will probably be very different. Perhaps you'll begin with small forays into the unknown, as you and your students experiment with inquiry-based learning; perhaps you'll start by engaging colleagues in a conversation about curricular fit, or begin developing a thematic unit together. Perhaps, as happened with me, your students will initiate the journey. Whatever the case, after you've sampled this "adventure guide" to science, the direction you take is up to you.

Bon voyage!

Properties of Water

My youngest students were fascinated by the physical properties of water; my older students were drawn to the creatures—real and imagined—who live in water. Because I had grown up by the ocean and had been lucky enough to participate in a whale research project, I had a slight head start in finding materials and information for these investigations. It was fun to extend my own understanding by tracking down these resources.

Properties of Water: Some Questions and Investigations

What sinks? What floats? Why can some things do both?
Why doesn't water go through my umbrella?
What colors can we make?
Can we make a river? Can we make it go up hill?
How does water get to the bathroom upstairs?
Is all the water (on earth) connected?
How does a toilet work?
Why do we have to save water? Why isn't there enough?
Let's put plumbing in the town we built!
Can the fish see out of the fish tank?

These questions led to investigations of a wide variety of subjects, including density, buoyancy, the water cycle, water pressure, hydrotechnology (pumps, etc.), boat design, consumer research on water use and conservation, absorption rates of various materials, geography and ocean mapping, navigation, weather, erosion, and the optical properties of water (bending light, magnifying, etc.).

Properties of Water: Materials

plastic tubs, many sizes
plastic and paper cups, many sizes
plastic eyedroppers (from drugstore)
plastic drinking straws
plastic cafeteria trays/meat trays (free or cheap from grocery store)
zip-lock bags, many sizes
miscellaneous objects to sink or float
clear plastic tubing (aquarium supply)
plastic drop cloths (from paint store)
plastic squeeze bottles from dish soap, shampoo, etc.

plastic film canisters (free from photo stores)
other nontoxic fluids to compare: cooking oil, corn syrup, etc.
aluminum foil
waxed paper
umbrella
fabrics, many kinds
paper towels
food coloring
hot pot
cooler (for ice cubes)
sand
coffee filters

Browse through your local variety store, hardware store, and supermarket to find many other useful materials to enhance your students' water investigation. Restaurants have big pickle jars and five-gallon plastic buckets that make great containers. Let parents know that you are beginning an investigation of water, and ask them to lend or donate items on your materials list.

Properties of Water: Books for Children

(The Dewey decimal classification for books about water is 551.)

Cobb, Vicki. 1986. *The Trip of a Drip*. Illustrated by Eliot Kreloff. Boston: Little Brown. Follow a water drop to find out about water treatment in this lively volume.

Cole, Joanna. 1986. *The Magic Schoolbus at the Waterworks*. Illustrated by Bruce Degen. New York: Scholastic. Ms. Frizzle and her class take a magic journey to find out how communities provide clean, safe water.

Reidel, Marlene. 1981. *From Ice to Rain*. Minneapolis: Carolrhoda. Children explore the role of water in the atmosphere, and its diverse forms.

Zubrowski, Bernie. 1981. *Messing Around with Water Pumps and Siphons*. Illustrated by Steve Lindblom. Boston: Little Brown. This paperback presents an array of fascinating ideas and activities for investigating water pressure and movement. Most can be done by children working alone; some might need supervision.

Properties of Water: Books for Teachers

Agler, Leigh. 1987. *Liquid Explorations*. Berkeley, Calif.: Lawrence Hall of Science (Great Explorations in Math and Science). Classroom activities and background information on properties of fluids.

Elementary Science Study. 1985. *Water Flow*. Nashua, N.H.: Delta. Classroom activities to investigate water pressure and movement, using plastic tubing and other inexpensive materials.

———. 1986. *Kitchen Physics*. Nashua, N.H.: Delta. Classroom activities using simple materials, with useful information for teachers.

———. 1986. *Sink or Float*. Nashua, N.H.: Delta. Classroom activities exploring density and buoyancy, adaptable to any age group.

Walker, Jearl. 1981. *The Flying Circus of Physics (With Answers)*. New York: Prentice Hall. Lots of puzzlers, some of which relate to behavior of water and other liquids. Explanations are detailed and sometimes difficult to understand, but still fun.

Westly, Joan. 1988. *Water and Ice*. Sunnyvale, Calif.: Creative Publications (Windows on Science). Primary classroom activities on the properties of water, in an easy-to-use format. Part of the excellent Windows on Science series.

The *World Almanac*, published annually and available at newsstands, has a directory of commercial and nonprofit associations. Included are the American Water Resources Association, the Water Pollution Control Federation, and the American Water Works Association, among others. These organizations might be able to help your students pursue specific lines of inquiry.

In addition to public libraries and bookstores, you might want to check the curriculum resource shelves of your district's science office, or visit the education library of a nearby college.

Properties of Water: Sources of Information and Assistance

Water Company. Your local utility probably has a budget and staff for developing and distributing educational materials on water, its use and conservation. Most companies will send free materials upon request; many will send a representative to visit with your class.

Plumbers. Check with your colleagues, parents, and neighbors to find a friendly plumber who will visit your class to talk about her work with water. Don't forget: Your school custodian might be a licensed plumber who would love to interact with students and faculty in this way.

Well Diggers. If some parts of your community use well water, then well diggers cannot be far away. Invite one to visit your class and share the process of finding and obtaining water from the earth.

Tailor, Cleaner, or Clothing Designer. Ask someone who works with textiles to come and explore with students the reactions of different fabrics to water.

Auto Mechanic. What do auto mechanics have to do with water? Don't wait till your radiator leaks to find out. Invite a mechanic to investigate the cooling properties of water with your students.

Physics Students. High school or college students in your community are probably studying the properties of water, too, and might enjoy a chance to interact with your students. Check with the physics departments to find out. (Some high schools and many colleges have student organizations dedicated to science and community service. Ask about these organizations when you call.)

Environmental Groups. If your school is located in a watershed or in a water conservation area, there might be a local environmental organization whose primary focus is water. Check the yellow pages to find a listing, or check with your state or local water resources division. Also, your local newspaper or radio station is a good source of information about local water issues and the groups actively involved.

State and Local Agencies. Your state's natural resources department is likely to have a water division. Write or call to find out what educational materials and programs they offer. Your local jurisdiction might have a similar agency.

Federal Agencies. The National Oceanic and Atmospheric Administration (Department of Commerce/NOAA, Education Program Branch, 11400 Rockville Pike, Rockville, Md. 20852, 301-443-8031) produces many excellent maps, posters, charts, and pamphlets about the oceans and weather. The U.S. Department of Agriculture Soil Conservation Service (USDA/SCS) also offers attractive and informative materials on the uses and conservation of water. Contact them through your local agricultural extension service. The Department of the Interior (DOI) oversees the River Basin commissions; there may be a commission established for a river near you. The Environmental Protection Agency (EPA) administers a water quality division, which might be able to provide materials appropriate for your students. Check the federal government section of your telephone directory for local DOI and EPA listings.

My students helped with the task of unearthing these resources. As part of their research on water, they wrote many letters explaining their projects and requesting information.

Properties of Water: Field Trip Sites

Bathroom or Kitchen (accompanied by a plumber). Invite a plumber (see above) to show your students what's inside a faucet, and how a toilet flushes. (Make sure to clear this "field trip" with the building custodian!)

Water Works. Many local water companies have tours for school groups. Students will see where water is collected, and how it is distributed to the homes and businesses of your community. Waste water treatment facilities might also be visited, to help students find out what happens to water after it goes down the drain.

Streams, Rivers, Lakes, and Ponds. If there is a body of water nearby, spend some time investigating it. Try to visit more than once, so children can observe changes in water level, see what happens as raindrops hit the water's surface, or note patterns in the water's movement.

Life in Water

Life in Water: Some Questions and Investigations

Does anything live in a mud puddle?
Tiny creatures appeared in our rain bucket! Where did they come from?
Do the same organisms live in fresh and salt water?
Why do they put seaweed in ice cream?
Are whales really endangered?
How do different kinds of water pollution (chemical, noise, etc.) affect
        different organisms that live in water? Are all plants and animals
        equally harmed?
Can we make a pond in the classroom?
When fish go to the bathroom, is it good for the water, or is it poisonous?
Is yeast a plant or animal? How does it stay alive in those little packets?
Why is there foam on the edge of a pond?

These questions led to many hours of making puddle and pond surveys; mapping; developing and using ecological inventories; acid rain and water quality testing; experimenting with drainage; testing soil absorption; constructing terrariums, aquariums, and "pondariums"; growing yeast to find out about population increase and requirements for survival; conducting consumer research on the ingredients in various brands of ice cream; using seaweed to make pudding and as sizing for handmade paper; identifying and estimating the population of humpback whales; and investigating the history and current use of Boston Harbor (a few blocks from school).

Life in Water: Materials

plastic tubs, many sizes
5- or 10-gallon aquariums or
    clear plastic shoe boxes
dip net or strainer
magnifiers
water
empty milk cartons, small and
    large

pictures from nature calendars or
    greeting cards
seafood menus
seafood and health food
    cookbooks
plastic bags
yeast

You can make a simple dip net by bending a wire coat hanger into a circular shape, and stitching or stapling the foot of an old nylon stocking to it. Or use an embroidery hoop to stretch a piece cut from the leg of a stocking.

An empty milk carton, small or large, makes a good pondside "holding tank" for organisms. Cut away the top, rinse the container well, dip a little pond water into it, and add whatever organisms the children collect. The tiny plants and animals will show up clearly against the white interior of the carton.

If you forget to bring magnifiers to the pond, simply fill a clear plastic bag with water, twist it shut, and look through it to magnify objects below.

Life in Water: Books for Children

(The Dewey decimal classification for books about life in water is 576.)

Ancona, George. 1990. *Riverkeeper*. Photographs by the author. New
    York: Macmillan. This slim volume chronicles the work of a

boatman who monitors the health of the Hudson River. The use of black and white photos lends a journalistic authenticity to the work.

Bunting, Eve. 1979. *The Sea World Book of Sharks*. Photographs by Flip Nicklin. San Diego: Sea World Press. Outstanding photos and interesting text about fascinating and often misunderstood fish. This book is considered to be one of the best available. Another excellent volume in the Sea World series is *Whales*, by the same author.

George, William. 1989. *Box Turtle at Long Pond*. Illustrated by Lindsay Barrett George. New York: Greenwillow. Through beautiful illustrations and simple text, young readers are introduced to the box turtle and other plant and animal inhabitants of the pond.

Holling, Holling Clancy. 1963. *Minn of the Mississippi*. Boston: Houghton Mifflin. Explore America's central waterway with this traveling snapping turtle. Look for other water-related stories by this author, including *Pagoo*, *Paddle to the Sea*, and *Seabird*.

Lane, Margaret. 1981. *The Fish: The Story of the Stickleback*. Illustrated by John Butler. London and New York: Collins. Richly illustrated with clear text about biology and behavior of a common fish.

McNulty, Faith. 1973. *The Great Whales*. Illustrations by Richard Cuffari. New York: Doubleday. An older book for intermediate readers, but still one of the best about these fascinating marine mammals.

Life in Water: Books for Teachers

National Aquarium in Baltimore. 1987. *Living in Water*. Baltimore: National Aquarium. Excellent activities for intermediate students; adaptable to younger children.

Niering, William. 1985. *Wetlands: An Audubon Society Nature Guide*. New York: Knopf. Excellent detail and color photos.

Outdoor Biology Instructional Strategies (OBIS). 1980–82. *Streams and Rivers Module*. Nashua, N.H.: Delta Education. Eight activity cards for outdoor learning experiences.

Ranger Rick's NatureScope. 1986. *Wading into Wetlands*. Washington, D.C.: National Wildlife Federation. Information, games, and investigations about wetland areas.

————. 1988. *Diving into Oceans*. Washington, D.C.: National Wildlife Federation. Information, games, and investigations about the sea.

Reid, George. 1967. *Golden Guide to Pond Life*. New York: Golden Press. An excellent, inexpensive little introductory guide.

Zim, Herbert S., and Hurst H. Shoemaker. 1956. *Fishes: A Guide to Familiar American Species*. New York: Golden Press. Another excellent, inexpensive little guide.

Life in Water: Sources of Information and Assistance

Colleges and Universities. Most colleges or universities offer at least one course, if not an entire program, in aquatic biology. Faculty members or students can be invited to visit your classroom to talk about and work with marine plants and animals. If a nearby college is part of the Sea Grant program sponsored by the National Oceanic and Atmospheric Administration (NOAA), they will provide specially designed educational programs and materials focusing on local aquatic ecology.

Fishing Enthusiasts. People who fish for fun or for a living are usually extremely knowledgeable about local aquatic habitats and the plants and animals occupying them. If you don't know anyone who fishes, check with your nearest sporting goods dealer, park manager, or scout leader. These sources probably know who would be a good "catch" for your classroom.

Aquarium Supply Stores. You can often get lots of help and information from people who sell fish and aquarium supplies. These experts can assist you in setting up a classroom aquarium of either native or exotic species. (They might also give you a classroom discount.)

Asian Market. The cuisines of China, Japan, Thailand, and other Asian countries are rich with the products of the sea, both animals and plants. A trip down the aisles of an Asian market will provide a range of canned and dried seaweeds, as well as an enormous range of edible sea animals to take back to the classroom.

Environmental Organizations. National and local organizations publish materials and sponsor many programs relating to the aquatic environment. Begin with your local Audubon Society or your state environmental education or science specialist to find out about organization listings.

Fish Marketing Association. If recreational or commercial fishing is an important industry in your state, there is probably a marketing association that publishes recipes, promotional posters, and general information on various local species. Check telephone listings for your state capital or the key fishing community, or consult your state's department of commerce for information on such local business associations. At the national level, the National Fish and Seafood Promotional Council, under the Department of Commerce, also offers materials about fish and fishing. It is located at 1825 Connecticut Avenue NW, Washington, D.C. 20009.

State Agencies. Most states have a department responsible for managing fisheries, either through natural resources, recreation, or commercial divisions. Check these offices for posters, curriculum materials, recipes, and educational programs.

Federal Agencies. The US Fish and Wildlife Service, part of the Department of the Interior, offers programs and materials relevant to almost every community in the country. Check phone listings for your local area or for your state capital. Also under the jurisdiction of the Department of the Interior are the following: the Minerals Management Service, which is responsible for environmental impact statements relating to offshore oil drilling and its effects on whales and other endangered species; the Center for Urban Ecology (1100 Ohio Drive SW, Washington, D.C. 20004), and the River Basins Commission (1100 L Street SW, Washington, D.C. 20001). The Department of Commerce and its National Marine Fisheries Service have several offices devoted to research and conservation. Among these are the Office of Fisheries Conservation and Management and the Office of Research and Environmental Information, both located at Colesville Road and East-West Highway, Silver Spring, Maryland 20910.

Life in Water: Field Trip Sites

Puddles, Streams, Ponds, Wetlands, Coastal Areas. Find out what bodies of water are most accessible to you and your students, then plan a visit to survey the site. Before collecting specimens to bring back to the classroom, be sure to check with your local Department of Natural Resources for information about protected species and water quality. (Some areas are quarantined for health reasons.)

Seafood Stores. A shop specializing in seafood or the fresh fish counter at your local grocery store offers a wide variety of inexpensive fish and shellfish species for students to examine. Bring a diverse assortment back to the classroom for dissection, fish printing, or a special feast. (Students might also enjoy the challenge of discovering which popular American food items—like ice cream and Worcestershire sauce—contain seaweed or fish products as ingredients.)

Seafood Restaurant. A class visit to a seafood restaurant can actually be a trip around the world, as students examine the menu for species (and recipes) that originate in near and distant habitats.

Archaeology

My students' curiosity about the people of the past provided a natural link between science and social studies. Were there cave men here? they wondered. How did the Indians know which plants were safe to eat? How did the Pilgrims keep those thatched roofs from leaking? These and other questions immersed third- through sixth-graders in reading, writing, experimentation, and field investigations in local archaeology.

Archaeology: Some Questions and Investigations

Were there really cavemen here?
Did cavemen cook?
If we don't have any caves around here, then where did people live?
How did they keep warm?
Where did they go to the bathroom?
How did the Native Americans know which plants were safe to eat?
How could one of these little arrowheads kill a great big bear?
Which trees were best for dugout canoes? Can we try making one?
Can a thatched roof really keep you dry?
All I keep finding is old, broken dishes. Didn't they do anything but eat back
      in the olden days?
What will people think about us a thousand years from now?

These questions led to investigations of the following subjects: fire and heat, architecture and building design, stonecarving, pottery making, buoyancy of various kinds of wood, water resistance of straw thatching, and construction of tools for hunting and fishing. Students conducted wastebasket "excavations," held schoolyard and backyard digs, and buried time capsules. They also buried a wide assortment of organic and manufactured materials to see which decomposed and which would remain for future archaeologists to unearth. In addition, they compared the effort and expense involved in catching fish using the ancient methods of Native Americans (Massachusetts and Wampanoag peoples) with modern costs and techniques.

Archaeology: Materials

trowels	crayons
plastic garbage bags	trash (not garbage)
newsprint paper	antiques or old junk

Archaeology: Books for Children

(The Dewey decimal classification for general archaeology is 913; for ancient peoples of the Americas, the classification is 930 or 970.)

Baylor, Byrd. 1969. *Before You Came This Way*. Illustrated by Tom Bahti. New York: Dutton. A strikingly illustrated walk back through time to the world of prehistoric artists. Look for other books by this eloquent author, including *When Clay Sings* and *One Small Blue Bead*.

Clark, Ann Nolan. 1941. *In My Mother's House*. Illustrated by Velina Herrara. New York: Viking. Award-winning classic tale of Southwest Indian life. My students compared the customs of its characters with those of our New England tribes.

Cobblestone. Cobblestone Publishing, 20 Grove Street, Peterborough, N.H. 03458. A magazine with stories and activities relating to American history for young readers.

Cork, Barbara, and Struan Reid. 1984. *The Young Scientist Book of Archaeology*. London: Usborne. Colorfully illustrated information and activities on archaeology, in an increasingly familiar comic-book format. Includes simple computer program for identifying a "pot."

Faces. Cobblestone Publishing, 20 Grove Street, Peterborough, N.H. 03458. An intermediate-level magazine of cultural anthropology, published in cooperation with the American Museum of Natural History.

Macaulay, David. 1984. *Motel of the Mysteries*. Illustrated by the author. Boston: Houghton Mifflin. An archaeological dig in the year 4022 unearths remains of the country of "Usa." Young readers have lots of fun imagining the ways that people of the future will interpret the traces of our time.

Porell, Bruce. 1979. *Digging the Past: Archaeology in Your Own Backyard*. Illustrated by Bruce Elliott. Reading, Mass.: Addison-Wesley. Intermediate readers will find this an excellent invitation to firsthand research.

Shemie, Bonnie. 1990. *Houses of Bark*. Illustrated by the author. Plattsburgh, N.Y.: Tundra Press. Detailed text and illustrations of Woodland Indian dwellings can serve as a guide for classroom or schoolyard constructions.

Smith, Howard E., Jr. 1989. *All About Arrowheads and Spearpoints*. Illustrated by Jennifer Owings Dewey. New York: Henry Holt. An intermediate-level examination of artifacts from prehistoric American cultures.

Tunis, Edwin. 1957. *Colonial Living*. Illustrated by the author. New York: Crowell. Detailed text and illustrations of the materials and customs of Colonial America. Look for other titles by this author, as all offer fascinating information and illustrations.

Wilbur, C. Keith. 1978. *The New England Indians*. Chester, Conn.: Globe Pequot Press. Incredibly detailed text and drawings of Woodland Indian tools, toys, and dwellings.

Archaeology: Books for Teachers

Ceram, C. W. 1971. *The First American*. New York: Harcourt Brace Jovanovich. A good introduction to the foundations of North American archaeology.

National Museum of Man 1979–present. *Canadian Prehistory Series*. Ottawa: National Museum of Man. Although this series is limited to an exploration of the archaeological sites of Canada, it provides excellent detail on modern archaeological findings and techniques and ways they relate to other disciplines.

Streuver, Stuart, and Felicia Antonelli Holton. 1979. *Koster: Americans in Search of their Prehistoric Past*. New York: Doubleday. An archaeologist and a journalist vividly describe the excavation of a site that was continuously inhabited from 7500 B.C. to A.D. 1200. This is probably one of the best basic introductions to the demanding but thrilling science of archaeology.

Archaeology: Sources of Information and Assistance

Colleges and Universities. Many schools offer at least one course, if not a whole program, in archaeology and anthropology. Faculty or students might be delighted to share their research and experience with the class.

Museums, Historic Homes, and Historical Societies. These institutions often have special programs and materials relating to local prehistory and history. They might also sponsor archaeological research in the surrounding community, and offer site tours or presentations about this work. Also, staff and volunteers or members of these organizations might be willing to work with your students in developing a schoolyard archaeological site.

State Archaeologist. Most states employ one or more archaeologists who are responsible for overseeing excavations and research on prehistoric and historic sites. They can provide listings of sites under study in your area, and might have educational materials as well. Many also invite public participation in excavations. Check state office directory, or consult your state's department of natural resources.

Local Planning and Zoning Administrators. Because so much of the United States was occupied, at one time or another, by prehistoric peoples, many communities have requirements about surveying construction sites and reporting findings of archaeological interest to local authorities before building begins. Your planning board should be able to advise you of your community's regulations and what sites are currently under consideration.

Archaeology: Field Trip Sites

A Wastebasket. Conduct an investigation in garbology by examining the contents of one day's trash from a "mystery classroom" or an unidentified home. How was the day spent at this site? What can you tell about the "culture" of this site, based on what its occupants threw away?

The Schoolyard. Use trowels and brooms to "excavate" a site on the school grounds. Is there an area near the dumpster where trash from "earlier times" has gotten covered over time? What lies hidden in the soil beneath the jungle gym, or around the softball field? (Be sure to let the principal or custodian know about your class excavations ahead of time. Wear protective gloves.)

A Vacant Lot or Construction Site. If there is a vacant lot or a site designated for construction near the school, you and your students might be able to explore it for signs of earlier occupation. (Be sure to get permission of the owners first. Track them down through neighbors, the local zoning office, or the registrar of deeds.)

Textiles

In the course of our archaeological studies, third- through fifth-grade students became interested in clothing, what it meant, and how it was produced by the various peoples who had occupied our area throughout history. They began to ask questions and conduct research about sheep and wool, tanning, weaving, and costume ornamentation, and eventually branched out from local research to cross-cultural studies. Why did the Egyptians wrap mummies in linen rather than wool? my students wondered. Why do people in tropical areas wear light-colored clothing? Are animal skins warmer than wool? Why don't nylon socks keep your feet warm?

Because I enjoy spinning, knitting, weaving, and sewing, it was fun to explore with my students the history, art, and science of textiles. It was also a great opportunity to team with a colleague who could share his expertise on vegetable dyes with the students.

Textiles: Some Questions and Investigations

Are light-colored clothes really cooler than darker ones? Why?
What fibers weave the warmest materials? Why?

How were the Native Americans able to weave waterproof baskets?

When you figure that the settlers had to raise the sheep and spend all that time making wool into cloth for clothing and blankets, were things really any cheaper back then?

If cabbage and Kool-Aid™ can color clothes, do they make my insides change color, too?

Which dyes wash right out, and which ones last? Why?

What makes fleece different from my golden retriever's hair? Why can I spin wool, but not this dog hair?

Is all animal hair "greasy" like wool?

Can we invent a better spinning wheel?

Some of these questions led into investigations of climate and living conditions of various regions. Some led to exploration of animal coverings, camouflage, and adaptations to climatic conditions. Others evolved into "chemistry" experiments with various dyestuffs. Still more delved back into water studies to examine permeability of different basketry fibers.

Textiles: Materials

cloth scraps, many kinds	string
yarns, many kinds	cardboard
fur and leather scraps	scissors
straws	thread

For Dyeing:

jars and tubs	onion skins, nuts, etc.
Kool-Aid™ (unsweetened)	alum (for colorfast dye)
cabbage, black beans	clothesline and pegs

For Fiber Experiments and Investigations:

cotton balls	weeds of many kinds
synthetic cosmetic puffs	hand lenses
wool fleece	microscope (optional)
pet hair (dog, cat, angora rabbit, etc.)	indoor-outdoor thermometers (for measuring insulation)

A very wide variety of small swatches of animal fur can be obtained from fishing supply companies, as fly-fishing enthusiasts use animal hairs to make their lures. L. L. Bean of Freeport, Maine 04033, offers a good selection that, we are assured, have been obtained from road-kills rather than hunting.

Textiles: Books for Children

(The Dewey decimal classification for books on textile crafts is 740, and for textile technology is 677.)

dePaola, Tomie. 1973. *Charlie Needs a Cloak*. Illustrated by the author. New York: Simon and Schuster. A classic for young children, and still one of the best descriptions of what it takes to make an article of clothing. Even my sixth-graders enjoyed this humorously illustrated story.

Francoise. 1951. *Jeanne-Marie Counts Her Sheep*. Illustrated by the author. New York: Scribner. Another classic for very young children; an early introduction to the economics of sheepherding.

Krumgold, Joseph. 1953. *And Now Miguel*. Illustrated by Jean Charlot. New York: Crowell. An award-winning intermediate-level story about a boy growing up in the sheep-farming Southwest. There is lots of detail to enhance students' understanding of the cycle from sheep to clothing.

Macaulay, David. 1983. *Mill*. Illustrated by the author. Boston: Houghton Mifflin. Intriguingly detailed illustrations and text about the construction and operation of one of America's first textile mills.

Miles, Miska. 1971. *Annie and the Old One*. Illustrated by Peter Parnall. Boston: Little Brown. This easy reader is about a young girl and her Southwest Indian grandmother, a weaver. An excellent opportunity for cross-cultural comparison of textile arts.

Robinson, Stella. 1984. *Textiles*. Illustrated by Derek Lucas. New York: Bookwright Press. A reference book for intermediate readers, highlighting a variety of familiar fabrics and the production process. My students used it to compare handcrafting with commercial techniques.

Schoop, Janice. 1988. *Boys Don't Knit*. Illustrated by Laura Beingessner. Trenton, N.J.: Africa World. Driven first by necessity, and then by delight, a little boy finds out that boys can—and do—knit. None of my boys were reluctant to get involved in textiles, but this is sure to help those that you might encounter.

Smith, Elizabeth Simpson. 1985. *Inventions That Changed Our Lives: Cloth*. New York: Walker. An intermediate-level, factual book, rather dryly written, but very useful as a reference.

Tunis, Edwin. 1965. *Colonial Craftsmen and the Beginning of American Industry*. New York: Crowell. Detailed text and illustrations about the many trades that supported colonial life-styles. (See Archaeology for listings of other excellent Tunis books.)

Wallace, Barbara Brooks. 1987. *Argyle*. Nashville: Abingdon. Illustrated by John Sandford. Argyle, a sheep, changes his diet and grows a colorful fleece, and delight soon turns to dismay! Children enjoyed this story as an accompaniment to their dye making.

Many cultures share tales and myths about spinning, weaving, sewing, and clothes. *Sleeping Beauty*, *Rumpelstiltskin*, and *The Emperor's New Clothes* are available in many print and film versions, as is the Greek tale of Penelope, the weaving wife of Odysseus. Compare the African *Anansi* stories with the Greek myths of Arachne, or check into Chinese folktale books for a fascinating perspective on textile arts and sciences in Asian culture.

Textiles: Books for Teachers

Alexander, Marthann. 1964. *Simple Weaving*. New York: Tower Books. A wide range of simple weaving techniques from many cultures, clearly explained.

Blumenthal, Betsy, and Kathryn Kreider. 1990. *Hands on Dyeing*. Loveland, Colo.: Interweave Press. Step-by-step guide to using home-grown and commercial dyestuffs.

Buchanan, Rita. 1989. *A Weaver's Garden*. Loveland, Colo.: Interweave Press. A horticulturalist identifies plants for weaving and dye sources; elaborates on plant properties and textile techniques.

Handwoven. Interweave Press, 201 East Fourth Street, Loveland, Colo. 80537. The May/June 1989 issue of this magazine is devoted to spinning, weaving, and dyeing with children, as well as to the history of children in the textile industry.

Kroncke, Grete. 1973. *Simple Weaving*. New York: Van Nostrand Reinhold. Instructions for many basic weaving techniques.

Liebler, Barbara. 1987. *Hands on Weaving*. Loveland, Colo.: Interweave Press. Step-by-step guide, from building a simple loom to weaving fabric.

Raven, Lee. 1988. *Hands on Spinning*. Loveland, Colo.: Interweave Press. Build a simple spindle and use it to experiment with different fibers to create yarn.

Shuttle, Spindle, and Dyepot. Handweaver's Guild of America, 998 Farmington Avenue, West Hartford, Conn. 06107. Lots of ideas and information in this magazine.

Threads. Taunton Press, 63 South Main Street, Newtown, Conn. 06470. A magazine devoted to both traditional and ultramodern fiber arts.

Textiles: Sources of Information and Assistance

Parents and Grandparents. Many children have relatives who are active hobbyists in the textile arts. Some might even have a family member involved professionally in some aspect of growing cotton, flax, or wool; spinning, weaving, and dying fibers; constructing clothing; or caring for finished textiles. These folks are eager to share their knowledge with the next generation. They're also a good source of scrap materials and loaned equipment.

Social Clubs or Church Groups. Clubs and church groups that represent specific ethnic traditions preserve and pass on many aspects of their cultural heritage. Members of these groups can engage students in diverse techniques for creating and finishing fabrics and costumes.

Crafts Clubs. Small sewing, knitting, and weaving groups exist all around the country. Members of these groups will visit classrooms to work with students; some groups will lend exhibits or equipment to schools. To find a guild near you, check with a local yarn or sewing shop, or consult listings in one of the magazines above.

High School Home Economics and Art Teachers. A nearby high school faculty might include an expert in textile arts and sciences. Teachers or students might be able to visit your class to teach techniques or to help with projects.

Textile Manufacturing Associations. The American Wool Council produces excellent posters and curriculum materials relating to wool and wool processing. For information, write to the Wool Education Center, 200 Clayton Street, Denver, Colo. 80206, or dial 1-800-USA-WOOL. The American Textile Manufacturers Institute, 1801 K Street NW, Washington, D.C. 20006 and the Northern Textile Association, 230 Congress Street, Boston, Mass. 02110, provide information on a wide variety of manufactured dry goods.

Textiles: Field Trip Sites

Fields and Meadows. Many weeds and woody plants can be used for creating textiles. Students can experiment to find out which plant fibers are strongest and most durable, then compare their findings to archaeological records. Which fibers work well for rope or string? Which can be woven into waterproof baskets? Are any soft enough for clothing?

Grocery Store. Dyes can be obtained from a wide variety of familiar products, including red cabbage, black beans, onion skins, walnuts, coffee, tea, and various berries. My students enjoyed identifying vegetable materials that are common in various regions of the world, then attempting to create authentic textile dyes.

Museums and Historical Societies. "Living Museums"—such as Colonial Williamsburg in Virginia, Connor Prairie Farm in Indiana, and Plimouth Plantation in Massachusetts—as well as local historical societies often maintain collections of early textiles from their communities. These organizations provide tours, presentations, and demonstrations of traditional techniques. The Museum of American Textile History, 800 Massachusetts Avenue, North Andover, Mass. 01845, has an extensive library and an impressive collection of materials and equipment tracing the development of textile processing in this country. The museum provides information and publications for educators, as well as programs for students from the region. The Textile Museum, 2320 S Street NW, Washington, D.C. 20008, has an enormous collection of textiles from Eastern Europe and Latin America. They also offer information and publications for educators.

Crystal Chemistry

One of my fifth-grade classes, enthralled by the latest science fiction adventure movie, was keen to study crystals. At first they were only interested in examining clear and geometrically perfect examples of quartz, fluorite, pyrite, and other "magical" minerals, and I doubted the study would last very long. Once the students began to cook up their own crystal recipes, however, their fascination grew and diversified. Even those committed to a more mystical perspective raised important scientific questions and pursued legitimate research.

Crystal Chemistry: Some Questions and Investigations

Where do crystals come from? Are they in lava?
Are there any crystals around here? Why don't all rocks have crystals?
You can't really eat crystals, can you?
Are there crystals on other planets?
If we put food coloring in the solution, will it grow colored crystals?
Are the crystals we made worth anything? Would crystals grow on other
        planets, or in the space shuttle?
Do crystals really have special powers?

These questions led to a range of investigations in chemistry and geology. Students dissolved crystals into solution; grew new crystals; studied maps and mineral guides to find geographical sources; revisited the previous year's volcano study to find out if any minerals crystallized from molten lava; experimented with heat, food coloring, and other variables to determine the effects of these factors on crystal growth. Students collected rocks from around their homes and the school and examined them to identify mineral constituents, experimented with mixed mineral solutions to see if they could grow their own rocks, checked grocery store shelves for edible crystals, designed a system for extracting salt crystals from seawater, examined beach sand in search of "minicrystals." They compared book, comic book, movie, and television representations of crystals; investigated the meanings of their birthstones; read myths and folktales from many cultures to find out what powers were attributed to crystals; investigated modern industrial and medical uses for minerals, studied NASA materials about the planets and their moons to find out about crystals in space.

Crystal Chemistry: Materials

clear plastic cups	hand lenses
plastic spoons	egg cartons
salt, sugar	plastic bags
epsom salt	baking soda
alum	Kool-Aid™
sand	ice cube trays
sandpaper	food coloring
cafeteria trays	

Check the baking supplies and spices section of your grocery store for crystals commonly used in cooking. (Children might need parental permission to wear or display birthstone jewelry.)

Crystal Chemistry: Books for Children

(The Dewey decimal classification for books on rocks and minerals is 550, and for chemistry is 540.)

Froman, Robert. 1967. *The Science of Salt*. Illustrated by Anne Marie Jauss. New York: McKay. This old book focuses on salt: its chemistry, commercial uses, and role in human physiology. The book offers information about chemistry and careers that is still quite useful, though somewhat stereotyped.

Srogi, Lee Ann. 1990. *Start Collecting Rocks and Minerals*. San Francisco: Running Press. Black and white photographs support an informative text, highlighting the identification, formation, and locations of crystalline minerals. A collection is included with the book.

Switzer, George. 1967. *Diamonds in Pictures*. New York: Sterling. Another old book, beautifully written by the chairman of mineral sciences at the Smithsonian, and worth seeking out on library shelves. It explains the formation, commercial procession, and uses of diamonds and discusses the development of synthetic diamonds.

Crystal Chemistry: Books for Teachers

Kincaid, Doug, and Roy Richards. 1983. *Earth*. London: MacDonald Learning Through Science. Distributed in the U.S. by Teacher's Laboratory. This packet of activity cards has many good ideas for working with soil, rocks, minerals, and crystals.

SAVI/SELPH. 1981. *Mixtures and Solutions*. Berkeley, Calif.: Lawrence Hall of Science. This activity packet is part of the excellent series, Science Activities for the Visually Impaired/Science Enrichment for Learners with Physical Handicaps. It contains guidelines for creating and comparing saturated solutions, from which crystals can be made.

Crystal Chemistry: Sources of Information and Assistance

Gem and Mineral Society. If no local group is listed in your phone book, hobby shop personnel might be able to recommend rock or mineral collectors in your area. These people are often eager to share their collections and expertise.

Jeweler. Artists who make metal or gemstone jewelry are knowledgeable about mineral crystals, their formation and use. Invite one from a local shop to visit your class and talk about these substances or a career with crystals.

Pharmacist. Your neighborhood pharmacy has an interesting variety of mineral crystals for use as home remedies. Check with the pharmacist to find out which are safest for classroom use.

College or University. Faculty or students in a local geology or earth sciences department may have made special study of crystalline minerals, and might be particularly knowledgeable about your local region.

State Geologist. Most states employ a specialist who is knowledgeable about local mineral resources; most also publish materials and even offer sample kits of local minerals. Check with your state's natural resources department or department of commerce.

Colleagues and Community. Let people know you are studying minerals, and donations of rocks, soil, and sand will quickly fill your science table.

Crystal Chemistry: Field Trip Sites

Schoolyard. Conduct a microtour of the playground, sandlot, field, or pavement, using a hand lens. Lots of crystals will turn up!

Kitchen or Health Room. Ask permission to take a guided tour of these shelves to find out what crystals you and your students use in daily school life. Supplement the activity by inviting students to bring assorted groceries or health and beauty aids from home. Read labels and compare ingredients with a mineral guide. (Bet you didn't know you brush your teeth with ground-up minerals!)

Railroad Tracks. The ballast, or broken rock, used along railroad tracks is often rich with crystal (and fossil) specimens. Check train schedules before visiting the site with your class, or gather specimens yourself for classroom use.

Beaches, River Banks, and Streams. Rocks and sand near waterways are often glistening with such crystalline minerals as mica, quartz, and garnet. Even along a short stretch of beach, the sand quality can vary considerably. Take several samples and make comparisons.

Deep Water Harbors. If your school is near a commercial seaport, you might be able to pick up scattered specimens of rocks that used to be carried as ballast by sailing ships. Students can examine them for presence of crystals and try to map their sources.

Discovery and Invention

Throughout their investigations, my students began to scrutinize more closely the assumptions that undergird much of classroom teaching and learning. "So the Indians taught the Pilgrims about gardening," one girl commented thoughtfully in the midst of our archaeological studies. "But who taught the Indians?" And during a navigation experiment, a fourth-grade boy wondered, "What good is a compass if you're lost? Just because you know which way is north doesn't mean you can find your way home!"

With questions like these, students began to probe the origins, evolution, and purpose of ideas. In some situations, we were able to stop and investigate on the spot. In other cases, we decided to record our questions and pursue them later. The assortment of delayed questions turned into a rather lively unit on discovery and invention. As you can imagine, there were lots of different projects going on at once. The most exciting aspect of this hodgepodge unit, from my point of view, was that the children, for the first time, began to see the human side of science, and to see their own potential as discoverers and inventors.

Discovery and Invention: Some Questions and Investigations

Why don't bicycles go backwards?
Who invented the compass? Why does it matter where north is?
Do you think there are any dinosaur bones here???
I figured out a way to put lights in my sister's dollhouse!
What if we put a motor on our paper airplane? Would it still fly? Would it
    go farther? Can we try?
I made a telescope just like Galileo's but it won't stay still, and all the stars
    keep jumping around. What can I do to fix it?
Did the Indians really invent fertilizer?
They're going to name an insect after me!
What about inventing a new kind of trap for cockroaches?
Aren't there any women inventors?

Discovery and Invention: Materials

toolbox
tape
batteries
water
cardboard
balloons
old machines for students to take
    apart (bicycle, eggbeater, etc.)

string
wire
magnets
flashlight bulbs
plastic tubing
wood scraps
straws
empty plastic bottles

Save (and ask parents to save) all kinds of household materials for use in inventions and investigations: egg cartons, toilet paper rolls, plastic or foil pans from frozen food, shoe boxes, film canisters, etc. Students will find many uses for these items!

Discovery and Invention: Books for Children

(Books on inventions can be found under Dewey decimal classification 608, and on exploration and discovery under 920. Be sure to check shelves under such specific subject headings as electricity, flight, biography, and so on, as well.)

Asimov, Isaac. 1972. *How Did We Find Out the Earth Is Round?* New York: Walker. This and other "How Did We Find Out" books by Asimov provide fascinating portraits of the process of scientific discovery and development of technological applications.

Billings, Charlene W. 1989. *Grace Hopper: Navy Admiral and Computer Pioneer*. Illustrated with photographs and prints. Hillside, N.J.: Enslow. Grace Hopper was a mathematician who helped design the first mainframe computer and was one of the few women to become an admiral in the U.S. Navy. (She is credited with first applying the term "bug" to a computer problem!) The text is a little dry, but the character is fascinating.

Caney, Steven. 1985. *Steven Caney's Invention Book*. New York: Workman. Steven Caney, who is well known among inventors for his creativity and knowledge, invites children to design, build, patent, and market their own inventions in this fat little paperback. Also included is information about important American inventions.

Jenkins, Gerald, and Magdalen Bear. 1987. *Sundials and Timedials: A Collection of Working Models*. Norfolk, England: Tarquin Publications. This paperback provides an assortment of timing devices to cut out, put together, and use. Information on the origin and use of the instruments is included, although the rather technical text might require some translation. Students can use the designs provided or expand on these ideas to create their own working timers.

Mander, Jerry, George Dippel, and Howard Gossage. 1967. *The Great International Paper Airplane Book*. New York: Simon and Schuster. This is an old book, but still the best on designing and building fabulous paper airplanes. No budding engineer should be without it.

Zubrowski, Bernie. 1990. *Balloons: Building and Experimenting with Inflatable Toys*. Illustrated by Roy Doty. New York: Morrow. Children can use a variety of common materials in combination with balloons to design toys and investigate forces and motions. Look for Zubrowski's many other outstanding books that encourage children to explore and invent.

Discovery and Invention: Books for Teachers

Abruscato, Joe, and Jack Hassard. 1977. *The Whole Cosmos Catalog of Science Activities*. Glenview, Ill.: Scott Foresman. This giant-size paperback is bursting with activity ideas, concise explanations of scientific principles, brief biographies of inventors and explorers, games, books, and other resources on many topics. My students found lots of ways to branch out and make their own discoveries after prowling through this volume.

Gould, Alan. 1986. *Hot Water and Warm Homes from Sunlight*. Berkeley, Calif.: Lawrence Hall of Science (Great Explorations in Math and Science—GEMS). This paperback activity guide offers information and ideas on designing, building, and testing solar-powered models. Like the other activity guides in the GEMS series, this provides a good starting point for many independent investigations.

National Science Resources Center. 1988. *Science for Children: Resources for Teachers*. Washington, D.C.: National Academy Press. This resource guide lists hundreds of curriculum materials, agencies, and information sources on almost every topic in the sciences. The directory of professional organizations is particularly helpful for locating individuals with ideas and expertise that can be shared with your class.

Olsen, Gary L., and Michelle J. Olsen. N.d. *Archi-Teacher: A Guide for Architecture in the Schools*. Chicago: Museum of Science and Industry. This paperback guide provides lesson plans and ideas for involving students in thinking about the purpose and design of the built environment. It's a good starting point for classroom investigation of structures and materials.

Westly, Joan. 1988. *Constructions*. Sunnyvale, Calif.: Creative Publications (Windows on Science). This early-childhood curriculum guide invites exploration of materials and construction of model buildings and machines. It's part of the excellent multivolume Windows on Science series.

Discovery and Invention: Sources of Information and Assistance

Invent America. U.S. Patent Model Foundation, 1331 Pennsylvania Avenue, NW, Washington, D.C. 20004 (202) 737-1836. This national, nonprofit organization provides materials and support for classroom invention programs, beginning with fostering creativity and problem-solving skills. They sponsor an annual conference for educators, and a contest in which as many as ten thousand elementary schools have participated.

U.S. Patent Office. 2021 Jefferson Davis Highway, Arlington, Va. 22201 (703) 557-3158. This federal agency, which issues patents for inventions developed and/or marketed in the U.S., offers educational films and brochures. If your school is near a Federal Depository Library (many colleges and universities serve in this capacity), you and your students can conduct patent searches to find out about interesting or unusual inventions.

American Association for the Advancement of Science. 1333 H Street NW, Washington, D.C. 20005, (202) 326-6620. This national organization sponsors many educational programs and materials and maintains regional networks of scientists who will visit classrooms to talk about their work. In addition to general programs, AAAS also provides special outreach related to women, ethnic minorities, and handicapped people in the sciences.

Chamber of Commerce. Your local chamber of commerce can provide information on businesses in your community who are involved in design and development of new products. Because the purpose of the chamber of commerce is to promote business, many branches support speakers bureaus through which you can invite guests to visit your class.

Historical Societies. These organizations often produce educational materials featuring early explorations of the local region or figures prominent in local history and commerce.

Colleges and Universities. Faculty and students in local biology, astronomy, physics, and engineering departments are often responsible for contributions to scientific knowledge in their fields. Some may have discovered new species of plants or insects in your community; others may be exploring the reaches of outer space. Invite these explorers to visit your class or to send reprints of their published articles.

Professional Societies. There are numerous national and local organizations of people active in the sciences and technology who can share their expertise with your students. Start with your phone directory, or use the National Science Resources Center guide (in teacher booklist, above) to locate these valuable resources.

Social Clubs or Church Groups. Members of these local organizations are often extremely knowledgeable about contributions made to science and society by others of their ethnic or cultural heritage.

Discovery and Invention: Field Trip Sites

Newspapers or Other Businesses. Many companies are happy to provide a guided tour of their facilities, explaining the history of their product and demonstrating mechanical processes. Parents are often excellent business resources.

Museums. Science museums are obvious repositories of information about scientific discovery and technological invention. Don't forget art museums, though: one of my classes conducted a scavenger hunt through a collection of American art, looking for examples of tools, machines, and scientific instruments depicted as background detail in portraits and landscapes.

Schoolyard. Students interested in exploration and discovery can begin by honing their observation skills in the classroom and schoolyard. Invent scavenger hunts and other observation games to get them looking carefully at their surroundings. (Entomologists agree that there are just as many new insect species to be discovered in our own backyards as in exotic locales!)

Antique or Junk Shops. You can find fascinating old gizmos at junk shops and flea markets. Students have lots of fun trying to figure out what purpose these items served or tracing the origins and evolution of the devices. If you can't take the class for a visit, a field trip through the pages of very old magazines or catalogs is equally intriguing.

Afterword

In the first chapter of this book, I discuss how important it is for teachers to write for teachers about matters of concern to teachers. My guess is that we have been successful, very successful, in this regard. That success, however, carries with it several dangers, dangers that can be avoided only if we remain aware and vigilant. All these perils have to do to some extent with expectations: community expectations for schools, school system expectations for teachers, and, most important, teachers' expectations for themselves.

The teachers with whom I have worked, as well as the teachers who are likely to read this book, are people with remarkably high expectations for themselves. Not only do they work hard in a daily way, but thoughts of their classrooms—children, methods, materials—often follow them as they drive their cars, take showers, or try to get to sleep. In short, teaching is a terrifically difficult, time-consuming, exhausting job.

Good teachers benefit from conversation and reflection: not just casual conversation but the kind of talk that helps people realize what they feel and believe. Only by putting ideas out there can we look back on them. Only by articulating our beliefs and our experiences can we find real, concrete moments to celebrate. Only by documenting the sources of our anxieties can we effect meaningful change.

This brings us back to the expectations issue. It seems inappropriate to me for teachers to add to their already burdened lives the expectation that they write for publication. Those familiar with classroom life know that there are many excellent teachers who do not write about their practice and have no desire to do so. In no way does this decision reflect on the quality of their work with children.

Teachers should, however, be expected to take the time to think about their activities. Schools need to provide time and space for teachers to consider what in their work is meaningful; what can be shared with other teachers, administrators, and the community; what ideas are worth revisiting; what practices might be changed. For the teachers who have contributed to this volume, writing has been helpful. And we encourage others of you to write—not only "How to Do X: A Practitioner's Perspective" pieces but also essays that make explicit the observing, questioning, and investigating that goes on in a vital classroom. Teachers are in a far better position than administrators or university researchers to explore day-to-day encounters with children. Ultimately, these are the insights on which instructional practices should be built. In addition, opportunities for engaging in conversations, sharing videos and other classroom materials, and exchanging visits, especially when supported by a school system, send out a clear message that reflection is valued. But to have these expectations imposed without adding resources is indeed a danger.

A second, related hazard has to do with changes in classroom practice. The teachers you have encountered in this volume have certainly made meaningful contributions to the intellectual quality of their own and their students' lives and have improved upon the "standard curriculum." On the other hand, it should be noted that all these practitioners have at least two kinds of support networks in place. First, they work in schools where their talent is recognized. Because administrators and fellow teachers value their insights and creativity, they see themselves as making contributions to the field of teaching even though they are sorely aware of the limitations of the environment in which school work takes place—overcrowding, too few resources, etc. In addition, they have all been involved with the Elementary Science Integration Project, a program funded by the National Science Foundation. The project has offered them both financial and collegial support for their classroom studies.

Two points emerge here. First, practitioners need backing if they are to effect change. Administrative praise for lesson or unit planning may be helpful, but even more valuable support emanates from a belief in a teacher's ability to think and develop and invent. People—teachers included—who feel they are under attack think defensively, not creatively.

By the same token, this sense that classroom educators can and do make a difference should not lead the general public or school administrators to expect teachers to shoulder the lion's share of school reform. For sanity's sake it is important that teachers recognize the difference between political problems (e.g., sufficient funding, changes in systemwide goals), which can be solved only through activity outside the classroom, and problems that can be alleviated through teacher attention and activity within the classroom. In other words, teachers need to choose their battles and their methods carefully. Not to do so ensures failure.

A final concern has to do with teacher talent. School systems often use expert practitioners to write curriculums or teach in-service courses, and it is certainly wise for administrators to seek expert involvement in such tasks. Frequently, however, teachers are asked to develop methods for teaching materials or concepts they have not chosen. In this sense they become technicians, delivering on someone else's blueprint.

By contrast, the work described in this book is original and self-directed. These teachers are not reporting on someone else's ideas or activities or problems. They write instead about their own annoyances and resolutions born from encounters with children and scientists. They have chosen to write for their peers in the hope of forming and joining a community in which teachers' intellects and imaginations are valued and the interests of children can best be served.

So we end this book with a smile and a bit of friendly advice. Start with yourself, your curiosities, your concerns. Think of your students as your colleagues. Together you know best how things work in your classroom, when and why you feel safe to take risks and share ideas. If you feel an observer would be helpful, invite administrators or university people into your classroom to help ask questions about what interests you. Get rid of the jargon; use *classroom* eyes and ears as the filter of activity. Let it make sense to your students and to you. Let *your* voices be heard.

Wendy Saul